2005

"An exceptionally comprehensive, well-researched study in its discussion of the economic and political failures of Marxism in Nigeria. With comparative insights, Hakeem Tijani provides a singularly significant contribution to the genre of studies that assess trajectories of leftist ideologies in the African Diaspora."

Juliet E. K. Walker,
Professor of History, University of Texas-Austin. Founder/Director, Center of Black Business, History, Entrepreneurship, Technology

"This book fills a critical gap in the intellectual history of nationalism in post World War II West Africa, and significantly contributes to the understanding of nationalist movements globally in the era of the 'Cold War.' Dr. Tijani has opened a new path towards the understanding of the impact of leftist ideology on anti-colonial movements in Nigeria. A well-researched study, the conceptualization is brilliant, the prose is elegant. The book is a matured piece of scholarship and its versatile relevance will ensure its lasting impact."

Akin Ogundiran,
Assistant Professor of History & Archaeology, Florida International University, Miami, Florida

"This is the first academic study on Marxist and other left-wing organizations that were active in Nigeria in the first two decades after the Second World War, presenting also the dimension of British response."

J. P. Brits,
Professor of History and Director of Postgraduate Studies, University of South Africa, Johannesburg, South Africa

AFRICAN STUDIES
HISTORY, POLITICS, ECONOMICS, AND CULTURE

Edited by
Molefi Asante
Temple University

A ROUTLEDGE SERIES

AFRICAN STUDIES
HISTORY, POLITICS, ECONOMICS, AND CULTURE

MOLEFI ASANTE, *General Editor*

KWAME NKRUMAH'S CONTRIBUTION TO
PAN-AFRICANISM
An Afrocentric Analysis
D. Zizwe Poe

NYANSAPO (THE WISDOM KNOT)
*Toward an African Philosophy of
Education*
Kwadwo A. Okrah

THE ATHENS OF WEST AFRICA
*A History of International Education at
Fourah Bay College, Freetown, Sierra
Leone*
Daniel J. Paracka, Jr.

THE YORÙBÁ TRADITIONAL HEALERS OF
NIGERIA
Mary Olufunmilayo Adekson

THE 'CIVIL SOCIETY' PROBLEMATIQUE
*Deconstructing Civility and Southern
Nigeria's Ethnic Radicalization*
Adedayo Oluwakayode Adekson

MAAT, THE MORAL IDEAL IN ANCIENT
EGYPT
A Study in Classical African Ethics
Maulana Karenga

IGBO WOMEN AND ECONOMIC
TRANSFORMATION IN SOUTHEASTERN
NIGERIA, 1900–1960
Gloria Chuku

KWAME NKRUMAH'S POLITICO-CULTURAL
THOUGHT AND POLICIES
*An African-Centered Paradigm for the
Second Phase of the African Revolution*
Kwame Botwe-Asamoah

NON-TRADITIONAL OCCUPATIONS,
EMPOWERMENT AND WOMEN
A Case of Togolese Women
Ayélé Léa Adubra

CONTENDING POLITICAL PARADIGMS IN
AFRICA
*Rationality and the Politics of
Democratization in Kenya and
Zambia*
Shadrack Wanjala Nasong'o

LAW, MORALITY AND INTERNATIONAL
ARMED INTERVENTION
*The United Nations and ECOWAS
in Liberia*
Mourtada Déme

THE HIDDEN DEBATE
*The Truth Revealed about the Battle
over Affirmative Action in South Africa
and the United States*
Akil Kokayi Khalfani

BRITAIN, LEFTIST NATIONALISTS AND THE
TRANSFER OF POWER IN NIGERIA,
1945–1965
Hakeem Ibikunle Tijani

BRITAIN, LEFTIST NATIONALISTS, AND THE TRANSFER OF POWER IN NIGERIA, 1945–1965

Hakeem Ibikunle Tijani

Routledge
New York & London

Published in 2006 by
Routledge
Taylor & Francis Group
270 Madison Avenue
New York, NY 10016

Published in Great Britain by
Routledge
Taylor & Francis Group
2 Park Square
Milton Park, Abingdon
Oxon OX14 4RN

Printed in the United States of America on acid-free paper
10 9 8 7 6 5 4 3 2 1

International Standard Book Number-10: 0-415-97812-2 (Hardcover)
International Standard Book Number-13: 978-0-415-97812-5 (Hardcover)
Library of Congress Card Number 2005021113

Library of Congress Cataloging-in-Publication Data

Tijani, Hakeem Ibikunle.
   Britain, leftist nationalists and the transfer of power in Nigeria, 1945-1965 / by Hakeem Ibikunle Tijani.
        p. cm. -- (African studies)
   Includes bibliographical references and index.
   ISBN 0-415-97812-2
   1. Nationalism--Nigeria--History--20th century. 2. Communism--Nigeria--History. 3. Nigeria--History--1900-1960. I. Title. II. Series: African studies (Routledge (Firm))

DT515.75.T55 2005
320.53'15'0966909045--dc22   2005021113

Taylor & Francis Group
is the Academic Division of Informa plc.

Visit the Taylor & Francis Web site at
http://www.taylorandfrancis.com

and the Routledge Web site at
http://www.routledge-ny.com

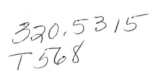

To God Almighty for His protection and glory all the time

Contents

Abbreviations

AG	Action Group
AMCONGEN	American Consul General
AMCONSUL	American Consulate
ANTUF	All-Nigerian Trade Union Federation
BC	British Consul
BDEEP	British Documents on the end of Empire
Brit. Empr.	British Empire
CACC	Christian Anticommunist Crusade
CO	Colonial Office
COMCOL	Commissioner of the Colony
CPGB	Communist Party of Great Britain
CPN	Communist Party of Nigeria
CSO	Chief Secretary's Office
DEFE	Defence Department (British)
DOS	Department of State (USA)
FGY	Federation of German Youth
HSU	Henderson State University
HTL	Harry Truman Library
HUAC	House Un-American Committee
ICFTU	International Confederation of Trade Unions
ICS	Institute of Commonwealth Studies
IJAHS	International Journal of African Historical Studies
ILO	International Labour Organisation
IUS	International Union of Students

JAH	Journal of African History
JHSN	Journal of Historical Society of Nigeria
JMAS	Journal of Modern African Studies
MRM	Moral Re-armament Movement
MSA	Mutual Security Agreement
NA	Native Authority
NAE	National Archive Enugu
NAI	National Archive Ibadan
NARA	National Archives and Record Administration
NCLC	Nigerian Christian Leaders' Conference
NCNC	National Council of Nigeria and the Cameroon (later National Council of Nigerian Citizens)
NCTUN	National Council of Trade Unions, Nigeria
NEPU	Northern Element Peoples Union
NLC	Nigeria Labour Congress
NMLHA	National Museum of Labour History Archive
NNSP	Nigerian National Socialist Party
NPC	Northern Peoples Congress
NPV	Nigerian Peoples Voice
NSUDIV	Nsukka Division (Nigerian Archive)
NUS	Nigerian Union of Students
NWU	National Women's Union
NYC	Nigerian Youth Congress
NYM	Nigerian Youth Movement
OAG	Officer Administering the Government (Nigeria)
OEA	Overseas Employers' Association
PCI	Peoples Committee for Independence
PREM	Prime Minister's Papers
PRD	Public Relations Department
PRO	Public Record Office
PSF	President's Secretary File (Harry S. Truman Library)
PTL	Pocket Testament League
RHL	Rhodes House Library
RIIA	Royal Institute of International Affairs
SWAFP	Socialist Workers and Farmers Party (Nigeria)

TUC	Trade Union Congress
UK	United Kingdom
UMBA	United Middle Belt Alliance
UNISA	University of South Africa
UPC	Union des Populations du Camerounais (Cameroon)
USA	United States of America
USF	University of St. Francis
USSR	Union of Soviet Socialist Republic
UWPP	United Working Peoples Party
WASN	West African National Secretariat
WFDY	World Federation of Democratic Youth
WFTU	World Federation of Trade Unions
WIDF	Women's International Democratic Federation (Prague)
WO	War Office (Britain)
WP	Working Party
WPCIPC	Working Party for the Colonial Information Policy Committee

Acknowledgments

To God is the glory! I would like to thank Professors Toyin Falola (University of Texas-Austin), Japie Brits (University of South Africa), Akin Ogundiran (Florida International University), and Juliet Walker (University of Texas-Austin) for reviewing chapter drafts. They offered useful comments that improved the quality of the work. Their views and constructive criticisms have greatly improved the quality of my presentation, style, and analyses. However, all pitfalls in this study are my sole responsibility.

To my wife, Olubunmi, I say thank you for the endurance spiritually, physically, and financially. My children (Funmi, Damilola, Tunde, Toyosi, and Gbolahan) endured several months of away from home, financial difficulty, and unusual schedule.

To my mentors, Professors Akanmu Adebayo and Adebayo Oyebade, I say thanks for various comments and assistance. I am also grateful to Drs. Angela Boswell, Hakim Adi, Phillip Zachernuk, Saheed Adejumobi, Simeon Ilesanmi, and Michael Ogbeidi of Henderson State University, Middlesex University, Dalhousie University, Seattle University, Wake Forest University, and the University of Lagos respectively. Professor Eileen Scully of Bennington College, Vermont deserves special thanks in all ramifications. Her comments and assistance are deeply appreciated. I say thanks to Mr. Benjamin Holtzman for facilitating the process of publication. To the series editor, Professor Molefi Kete Asante, I say thanks for all the comments.

Lastly, the staffs at the PRO, NARA, NAI, UNISA library, Henderson State University library, and the Social Science Department secretary at Henderson State University are supportive and I thank them. The University of St. Francis, particularly Professors Jeff Chamberlain, Cathy Schultz, Connie Bauer, Frank Pascoe, Julie Victa, and President Michael Vinciguerra provides excellent atmosphere for review and completion of the manuscript. To Lookman Adio and Liba Oridedi, I say thanks for accommodating me during several visits to NARA in Maryland. To almighty God, I say thank you for giving me the fortitude to meet the high standard required by all.

Hakeem Ibikunle Tijani, PhD
USF, Joliet, Illinois, 2005

Chapter One
The Preamble

THE STATE OF KNOWLEDGE:
UNDERSTANDING THE LITERATURE

In contemporary world politics, Marxism-Leninism has provoked an enormous outpouring of literature ranging from academic to propagandist. The more academic and historical works may be classified under country studies, comparative cases, and critiques of both the ideology itself and the various revolutionary movements it inspired in both Europe and the Third World.[1] While there are many solid country studies and comparative works on nationalism and decolonization in Asia, Africa, and the Middle East, there is no comprehensive study about the development of leftist ideology and organizations in Nigeria itself between 1945 and 1965. The otherwise pioneering works of Coleman, Olusanya, and Sklar offer valuable overviews of political development and nationalist struggles in Nigeria but ascribe little significance to the long history of leftist ideology in the region; as well, they do not fully appreciate the deep inroads radical leftists made into mainstream nationalist organizations.[2]

The works of Ajala, Esedebe, Langley, Legum, Nkrumah, and Padmore focus on the general Pan-African use of some of the ideals of communism as the basis of nationalist struggle in Africa. Alade, Ikoku, Madunagu, Osoba, Waterman and Zachernuk discuss the African intelligentsia's ideological orientation.[3] Narasingha, on the other hand, compares the role of the Left during the colonial and post-colonial period, concluding "socialism holds an uncertain prospect for the future of Nigeria."[4] Frank, in his 1979 essay "Ideological Competition in Nigeria: Urban Populism versus Elite Nationalism" analyses the nature of ideology in Nigeria and relates ideological competition to conflict between Federal and local interests.[5] In his study Olakunle Lawal identifies the significance of radical nationalism but fails to discuss the Marxist ideological undertones of this radicalism. This shortfall is partly filled by Siyan Oyeweso in his study of Mokwugo Okoye.[6] Abdul Raheem and Olukoshi, Falola and Adebayo, Eze, Okoye, and Uyilawa present a narrative of the left wing and socialist struggle in Nigeria. Their studies are useful tools for a more meaningful analysis. In a separate study, Falola gives an in-depth account of colonial development planning and decolonization in Nigeria, and his work remains a vital source for understanding anti-socialist measures in colonial developmental plans.[7]

Awa, in his 1964 *Federal Government in Nigeria*, narrates the political history of the country by examining various constitutions and the workings of the government. In another study, he focuses on the place of ideology in Nigerian politics, identifying three distinct strands: nationalism, capitalism and socialism. On nationalism, Awa concludes, "although the nationalist movement increased the momentum of the agitation for independence, it did not evolve any ideas that could help develop consensus in the country." According to Awa, "[m]ost leaders in Nigeria favoured capitalism to [i.e., over] socialism." To him, "socialism has not made a great impact on the society in practical terms because, there are many strands to the ideology. Its votaries have tended to dissipate energy fighting one another and not the primary adversary, namely, poverty, and those who perpetuate it." Another reason he gives is that the "principal spokesmen for socialism at one time or the other abandoned the cause and either went over to the capitalist camp or remained neutral in the ideological debate."[8]

In separate studies, Aluko, Kirk-Greene and Phillips offer insights into the evolution and development of the Foreign Service and foreign policy in Nigeria, as well as into the leadership's ideological leanings. Aluko and Kirk-Greene agree that the evolution of the Foreign Service should be dated back to 1950, when the process of Africanisation was in full throttle. Both, however, fail to identify ideological undertones in the evolution and development of the Nigerian Foreign Service during the period. Phillips narrates the emergence of a non-neutralist foreign policy on the eve of independence. He discusses the place of ideology and the East-West politics as a campaign issue during the 1959 general elections.[9]

Writing in the mid-1960s, Apthorpe, Bhambri, Dudley, Omer-Cooper and Post were concerned about the progress and prospects of Marxism in Nigeria. *The Nigerian Journal of Economic and Social Studies* published various papers from a symposium held in July 1964 at Ibadan, where scholars gathered to discuss Marxian ideas and social progress in Nigeria. In his contribution, "Marxism and Political Change in Nigeria," Dudley concluded that Marxism succeeded only insofar as the Marxists were willing to cooperate with the bourgeoisie. "That is why," according to him, "independent Nigeria emerged with a ruling governing class recruited mainly from the intelligentsia and the bourgeoisie." Omer-Cooper in his "Nigeria, Marxism and Social Progress," concluded that, "if taken . . . as a scheme to be applied dogmatically to circumstances so different from those which inspired its authors—it could only lead to illusion and conceal the real problems of social progress in Nigeria."[10] Apthorpe focused on Marxism and law in Nigeria, concluding that Marxian ideas do not fit into Nigerian law, nor were they wholly applicable. Bhambri, in his "Marxist Economic Doctrines and their Relevance to Problems of Economic Development of Nigeria," maintained that Nigeria could not afford to be aligned with the Soviet bloc. As he put it, "dependency on the communist countries is likely to expose the Nigerian economy to more dangerous forms of instability."[11]

More recent studies have examined the extent to which ideology influenced nationalist and labor leaders. An account of the significant role of the Zikist Movement in the nationalist struggle in Nigeria is found in the works of Iweriebor and Tijani. Iweriebor, in particular, claims that, "under Eze and Okoye, the movement's political orientation and discourse had acquired a definite socialist inflection." Tijani goes further, identifying the extent of Marxist influence in the struggle against British officials and conservative nationalists.[12]

Ananaba, Akpata, Cohen, Cowan, Otobo, Egboh, Melson, Tokunboh and Yesufu have opened new avenues of inquiry in their studies of Nigerian trade union movements. Ananaba in *The Trade Union Movement in Nigeria* gives a lucid account of Labor politics in colonial and post-colonial Nigeria. In his larger study, *The Trade Union Movement in Africa*, he provides insights into the evolution of labor movements in Africa generally. Akpala emphasizes the evolution of trade union movements in Nigeria and attempts after 1945 to institute educational programs for unionists.

Cohen in his *Labour and Politics in Nigeria* discusses the history of labor movements in Nigeria, emphasizing the role of international labor politics in the split of union leaders. Cowan traces the history of trade unionism worldwide, highlighting its role in nationalism. Egboh's studies are mainly about the origin of trade unionism and its problems and prospects during the colonial period. Otobo, in his various studies on labor relations and trade unions in Nigeria, provides valuable information in this regard. In *Foreign Interest and Labour Unions in Nigeria* and *State and Industrial Relations in Nigeria*, he gave a clear account of the origin and growth of the labor movement in Nigeria but with only passing reference to the Communist International's support for labor movements. As with earlier authorities, he does not adequately address the perceived communist threat as it related to decolonization; similarly, he does not discuss various anti-Communist measures taken by British officials and leading nationalists in Nigeria as part of an effort to establish pro-Western labor organizations in colonial and post-colonial Nigeria. Melson narrates ideological failure of the 1964 labor strike and its implications on Marxist groups. Tokunboh in *Labour Movements in Nigeria: Past and Present* also provides a lucid account of the emergence and development of trade unions in Nigeria. To Yesufu, modern industrial relations in Nigeria cannot be divorced from trade union agitation since the colonial period.

Some scholars and government functionaries have carried out research about Communist infiltration of the trade union movements in the colonies generally. Although some of them might have been influenced by their ideological orientation, they nonetheless provide useful accounts about the role of Communism, Socialism and the Cominform in metropolitan and colonial trade unionism. In this category are the works of Friedland, Gonidec, Laybourn, Lichtblau, Nelkin, Roberts, Zakharia and Magigwana.[13] Adi, Callaghan, and Howe have individually analyses the role of the British Left in colonial politics. Stephen Howe in his *Anticolonialism in British Politics: The Left and the End of Empire, 1918-1964,* analyses the role of the Left with emphasis on the Communist Party of Great Britain, the Labour Governments, and the Movement for Colonial Freedom, within the context of colonial politics. Adi in "West Africans and the Communist Party in the 1950s," highlight the relationship between Nigerian students in Britain during the 1950s and the leadership of the Communist Party of Great Britain. This is further expanded in his doctoral thesis "West African Students and West African Nationalism in Britain, 1900–1960." And in "The Communist Movement in West Africa," he concludes, "clearly the history of communism in West Africa has still to be written." To Adi, "there is much to indicate that it was a significant ideology which exercised an important influence on individuals and the anti-colonial and labour movements." Callaghan is concerned with the role of the British Communists during the World Wars in promoting pro-Allied efforts with the hope of a socialist triumphal or at least the Labour Party momentum after the war.[14]

Ronald Hyam's documentation of the Labour Governments and the end of the British Empire is another useful lead. He suggests that between August 1945 (after VJ-Day) and September 1951 (before handing over to the Conservative Party) the issue of containing communism was paramount in Labour government international relations policy. Despite some Left-wing ideologues in the Labour Party, the government was not tolerant of Marxist-Leninist ideals in its policy formulation. Thus he concludes that the foundation of an anti-Communist policy in British strategy was the product of the two post-World War II Labour Governments.[15]

David Goldsworthy, in his volumes on the Conservative Governments, notes that "Africa South of the Sahara was far from un-important" in Cold War politics. He notes that the Conservative Governments, like their Labour predecessors, were concerned about the growing influence of Nasser's Egypt, and with it, Soviet influence in spreading communism in Africa. He also asserts that the U.S. was concerned about the menace, which led to its floating the idea of a "committee of American, British, French, and perhaps Belgian officials to consider how best to combat Soviet subversion in Africa."[16] The basis for this U.S. initiative is well covered in Oyebade's "Feeding America's War Machine."[17] More generally, the collapse of the Soviet bloc in the final decade of the twentieth century and the opening of Russian archives have confirmed earlier understandings of Soviet interest in Africa south of the Sahara. The exploration of post-independence relations between Nigeria and the USSR, up until the collapse of the Soviet Union in 1991 is contained in Maxim Matusevich's recent work.[18] The classic and still invaluable analyses of Soviet activities among black Africans remains Edward Wilson's 1974 study, in which he argued that "Russian involvement had begun in Africa long before the Second World War and had strong historical roots." In this pioneering work, he maintained, "Having failed to establish colonies of her own, Russia adopted a policy of preventive imperialism, attempting to deny other powers what she herself could not have."[19]

Autobiographies and biographies are also useful tools in reconstructing the history of leftist ideology and organizations in Africa, Nigeria in particular, but there are distinct limits to participants' own understanding of larger events. For example, autobiographical works by Ahmadu Bello, Obafemi Awolowo, Anthony Enahoro and Sir Bryan Sharwood Smith mention only in passing the appeal of leftist and Marxism-Leninism in Nigeria.[20] Amechi, Davies, Foot, Mbadiwe, Nzimiro and Osita do not give detailed accounts of the role of the Soviet Union and the Communist International in their memoirs, emphasizing instead the evolution and ideals of Zikism.[21] In a work that does provide a general description of Communism and the state, Nnamdi Azikiwe underscores the role of a few notable communists in post-independence Nigeria, but concludes from a participant's vantage point that: "communism is suitable for adaptation but not for adoption in Nigeria."[22]

A review of relevant biographical and autobiographical literature would not be complete without studies about Tafawa Balewa, one of the leading nationalists of the period and of course the person to whom the governance of Nigeria was entrusted on October 1, 1960. Trevor Clark narrates his role first as the Leader of Government Business, and later Prime Minister of the Federation of Nigeria. In relation to this study, Clark and Epelle have separately discussed the role of Balewa in nationalist politics as well as his role in the decolonization era. Like Nkrumah (1948–1957) in the Gold Coast and Tunku Abdul Rahman in Malaya, Balewa did not hide his distaste for leftist ideologues. This study will elaborate on his significant and unique role in the formulation and execution of anti-leftist policies in the 1950s through 1965.[23]

CRITIQUE OF SOURCES

The study draws upon official and unofficial materials available in England, Nigeria, and the United States of America. Also important for accurate and lucid analyses of events, issues, and personalities are personal papers and newspaper reports in various archives and libraries in these countries. More particularly, newspaper reports and private memoirs provide useful information for the reconstruction of the Zikists' ideological orientation, activities of the Special Branch, and the colonial police. Records at the CPGB and the Trade Union Congress (TUC) corroborate newspaper reports and some official intelligence reports relating to the presence of some Nigerian Marxists and their orientation towards the CPGB "British Road to Socialism." The CPGB files also confirmed colonial and nationalist government anxieties about the activities of these men who tried to form a nation-wide Marxist-Leninist movement in the 1950s.

In the Public Record Office (PRO)—now National Archives, London, the files of the Cabinet and its committees, Colonial and Foreign Offices remained the main source of information. Records from the U.S. National Archives and Record Administration, Maryland complement this PRO material. In Nigeria, the regional archives in Ibadan and Enugu provided information concerning British administrators and their Nigerian counterparts during the period; especially valuable are the chief secretary's file, divisional records, and intelligence reports by field officers. Various government reports and annual reports of some departments (Labour, Information and Research, and the Police) have been quite useful. Also, government publications such as Notices, Gazettes, Council of Ministers' Minutes and Parliamentary Debates provided useful information. Of the many valuable Government publications in the UK, perhaps the most significant of all was His (later Her) Majesty's Stationery Office Publications entitled *Colonial Annual Reports.* The series on Nigeria entitled, *Nigeria: Colonial Annual Reports,* covered the 1920s to 1960.

Lastly, important gaps in these other materials were filled using materials from the Moral Re-armament Archives, Cheshire and Victoria; the British Trade Union Congress (TUC) Collections, University of North London, British TUC Registry Files at the Modern Record Centre, the University of Warwick, as well as the Communist Party of Great Britain Papers at the National Museum of Labour History Archive Centre, Manchester.

ANALYZING THE CHAPTERS

There are nine chapters in this book. Chapter One is a general introduction, emphasizing the basis and relevance of studying the development of leftist ideology and organizations in Nigeria. In Chapter Two we identify the significance of a comprehensive study about the development of Marxist ideology and organizations in Nigeria during the colonial and post-colonial periods.

Chapter Three is an assessment of the role of Zikist movement in Nigeria with emphasis on the degree of Marxian ideological influence. It analyses why and how radical youths adopted Marxian ideology in their struggle against British colonialism in Nigeria. Their radical ideology marked a departure from the hitherto peaceful demand by nationalists for devolution.

Chapter Four is about attempts at regrouping after the colonial government ban on the Zikist movement in 1950. It is an account of leftist reformation, regroup, and future of the ideology and organizations in Nigeria. This chapter is a comprehensive analysis of "communism within," emphasizing the role of Marxists and their sympathizers in nationalist movements and labour unionism. It reflects upon Nigerian attempts to adopt Marxist-Leninist ideology to a colonial situation. The official CPGB perception of their activities is also detailed.

Both Chapters Five and Six complement one another. Chapter Five is a profile of notable Marxists during the period under study. While the list is selective, the chapter highlights further their roles, goals, aspirations, and disappointments. Chapter Six addresses a major initiative on the part of the McPherson, Balewa, and Robertson administration with regard to the employment of leftist ideologues. It also discusses how the private sector and the main political parties ostracized the Marxists in political and economic affairs. Here detail about British colonialist sanctions, measures, and co-optation as hegemonic responses to the insurgent Marxist groups is provided. Chapter Seven explains the collaboration between Nigerian government and France as a neighboring colonial power; sharing of intelligence and general co-operations between Anglo-French officials is discussed with recently declassified materials from the Public Record Office, London. The important role of the United States in combating leftist ideology worldwide, and particularly in the most populated British colony of Nigeria is discussed. There is now evidence that U.S. officials were deeply concerned with events in British West Africa, and gathered intelligence both covertly and overtly that were used to combat leftist menace. On the other hand, the book queried the sincerity of U.S. (government and non-government projects) development plans for colonial territories after World War II and its economic collaboration with the colonial office.

Chapter Eight is a reflection upon embattled leftists and their quest for a place in an independent Nigerian state, emphasizing in particular leftist reactions to the process of British devolution. The role of Marxist groups between 1960 and 1965 in the new nation is also discussed. In Chapter Nine, which is also the conclusion, we identify plausible reasons for the failure of Marxian ideology and organizations in Nigeria.

In summary, a history of leftist ideology and organizations in Nigeria during the decolonization era up to 1965 is relevant. An understanding of this aspect of Nigerian history will illuminate our reflections on how and why the aspirations of the Marxists (and their sympathizers) remained elusive since independence in 1960. It also explains why the Nigerian nation is pro-Western in all spheres of life.

Chapter Two
Ideology of the Left in Colonial Territories

INTRODUCTION

The potent mix of decolonization, anti-imperialist indigenous nationalism, and Marxism-Leninism first came to regions under European colonial control in the years immediately following World War I. At the treaty talks at Versailles formally ending World War I and establishing the League of Nations, American President Woodrow Wilson's calls for a new world order built upon collective security and national self-determination inspired anti-colonial nationalist groups across Asia and the Middle East.[1] The terms of the final treaty, however, deeply disillusioned and embittered these nascent nationalists in the colonies. The new world order limited the right of self-determination to European areas of the former Austro-Hungarian empire, reaffirmed European colonial interests across the globe, and handed over Germany's imperial holdings in China to Japan, the most recent arrival among the great powers.

MARXISM-LENINISM AND ANTI-COLONIAL NATIONALISM

Marxism-Leninism emerged amid this disillusionment as a radical alternative to the post-Versailles world order.[2] The revolutionary theory offered indigenous nationalist leaders a coherent critique of imperialism as an outgrowth of capitalism, an understanding of capitalism as a flawed, self-destructive phase in human history, together with a vision of post-colonial, anti-Western modernization. The Marxist component of this ideological mix, enunciated in the mid-19th-century collaborative writings of Karl Marx and Friedrich Engels, was a normative theory of history, a radical socialist brand of political economy, and a call for international proletarian

9

struggle against bourgeois capitalism. The Leninist component grew out of the Bolsheviks' successful revolt against tsarism in Russia in the closing years of World War I. Leninism offered a blueprint for revolutions, calling for a small, highly disciplined party to form the 'vanguard of revolution,' forge coalitions of convenience with class enemies, and employ violence to achieve revolutionary ends.

This hybrid Marxism-Leninism gained ground internationally when the newly established Union of Soviet Socialist Republics (USSR), repudiated tsarist treaties concerning colonial arrangements and nationalized foreign investments and properties in Russia. Bolshevism in power became synonymous with "the theory of the party as a dedicated revolutionary order, the tightening regime of party discipline, the absolutism of the party line, the intolerance of disagreement and compromise, and the manipulative attitude toward mass organisation."[3] Ironically, as Britain and France moved to liberalize their colonial administrations, this loosening opened up avenues of access for Soviet ideological and material influence.

After World War II, decolonization and independence movements swept through Asia, the Middle East, and Africa. Once again, the words of an American president had inspired calls for self-determination, and once again, post-war realities fell far short of wartime rhetoric and promises. Franklin Delano Roosevelt, together with England's Winston Churchill, had issued the "Atlantic Charter" in 1941, framing the war as a struggle for the principle of universal self-determination and the end of imperialist economic arrangements. While Roosevelt and Churchill had their own agenda, there is no doubt that the echoes of Woodrow Wilson's promises provided an opening for anti-colonial nationalist groups; the leading Nigerian nationalist spokesman Nnamdi Azikiwe used a visit in London in 1943 to hand-deliver to the colonial secretary a memorandum entitled, "The Atlantic Charter and British West Africa," demanding independence within fifteen years.[4]

In the immediate post-war years, however, both Britain and France refused to relinquish their colonies, and the American commitment to anti-imperialism was compromised by its growing alarm over Soviet territorial gains in Eastern Europe and apparent Soviet ideological gains in the Third World. Seeing colonial resources and markets as essential to Western European postwar recovery, the U.S. muted its opposition to French and British empire-salvaging efforts. At the same time, the Soviet Union's emergence as a counterweight to Anglo-American power meant that Marxism-Leninism gained force and legitimacy as an ideology and blueprint for mobilizing anti-colonial indigenous nationalist groups.

The decades between the Bolshevik takeover of Russia and the post-World War II push for decolonization had broadened and complicated

Marxism-Leninism. To Lenin's party dictatorship, his successor Joseph Stalin contributed to the mix and insistence upon the infallibility of party leaders, a single-party system in a totalitarian state, a command economy to achieve 'socialism in one country,' the cult of personality, a reign of terror built on institutionalized violence, intrusive Soviet domination over neighboring communist parties, and Soviet ideological hegemony within the world-wide communist movement.

Communist revolution in China, culminating in the creation of the People's Republic of China in 1949, legitimized Maoism as an alternative road to socialism in non-industrialized, overwhelmingly peasant societies.[5] Although closely tied to the Soviets, the Chinese Communist Party embraced Maoism as an alternative road to socialism, and China emerged as an ideological rival for leadership in the international communist movement. China's example made it possible for socialist or communist parties to pursue alternate roads to revolution, acknowledging two types of conflict: the first, so-called "non-antagonistic contradictions" among socialist powers and within communist parties, to be resolved through fraternal discussions and self-criticism; the second, "antagonistic contradictions," between the proletariat and the bourgeoisie or the ruling elite, resolvable only through revolution.[6] Within the Soviet bloc, Josip Tito demonstrated the utility of communism in uniting a country whose boundaries had been imposed by outside powers. Both Titoism and Maoism came to represent a socialist road avowedly independent of Soviet domination, a feat made ever more difficult in the hardening bipolarity of the Cold War.

LEFTIST IDEOLOGY AND ANTI-COLONIALISM IN BRITISH AFRICA

In World War I, colonial powers' reliance upon local African economies and work force, combined with greater prosperity and professionalization among intermediaries and Western-educated Africans, increased pressures to liberalize colonial administrations. In areas with dense white settlement, such as Southern Rhodesia, British colonial reforms were too slow for black Africans but too radical for white residents. London's consequent stepping-back from pledges radicalized nationalist groups, leading in turn to greater British rigidity. The rhetoric of self-determination, given a pan-African focus by W.E.B. DuBois and the political sophistication of African students returning from British universities, mobilized elite Western-educated Africans, seen for example in the 1918 formation of the National Congress of British West Africa, and in the mid-1920s, of the West African Youth League, and the Nigerian National Democratic Party.[7]

However, in Africa generally and West Africa more particularly, inter-war anti-colonialism was "incipient rather than openly challenging."[8] Three coherent groups emerged in West Africa as players in resistance to colonial rule. Tribal leaders and traditionalists tended to accommodate British authorities in exchange for the status quo; a professional, commercial elite—many with family ties to tribal chieftains—identified with things British and sought to negotiate higher status and some liberalization of colonial government; a third element comprised a nascent urban-centered activist elite with connections to the British left, sharing a dawning recognition that colonial reform would never go far enough, and might even be a hindrance to complete independence.[9]

In the late interwar years, and through the early 1940s, the second and third of these three pivotal groups emerged to dominate nationalist and decolonization movements, often as rivals, but also as powerful pressure groups against British colonial rule. During the war, various political groups representing the second element coalesced to demand self-government—the National Council of Nigeria and the Cameroon, the Nyasaland African Congress, and the Kenya African Union—inspired by the model of the Indian Congress Party. However, changing economic and demographic factors forced such groups to undertake mass mobilization or be left behind as a vestige of colonialism.

A wartime boom, coming out of the demands on colonial markets to supply British and American troops, and the disruption of British trade routes elsewhere enhanced the economic and political power of native farmers and middlemen. Returning war veterans, overseas African students, and a self-conscious professional class, took hold of nationalist parties, pushed for expanded access to education, and established trade unions. The infrastructure laid down to move troops and supplies in wartime now provided avenues of contact and mobilization beyond and between cities. Growing urban populations organized against price increases in consumer goods and against colonial rule more generally, as in the 1945 general strike in Nigeria, and the 1948 riots in Accra.[10]

In post-World War II Africa, then, the pathways to independence among nationalist movements ranged from western-oriented groups employing Mohandas Gandhi's non-violent resistance strategy, to national liberation united fronts relying upon guerrilla tactics.

In colonial Nigeria, both external and internal pressures contributed to the growing strength and visibility of the more militant nationalist organizations. The Nigerian Youth Movement (1934) and National Council of Nigeria and the Cameroons (1943) mounted continued criticism of colonial administration and demands for a constitutional roadmap to self-rule—

demands for more native participation in a reformed colonial administration.[11] These groups were "urban based, led by the educated elite who operated through ethnic unions within the municipalities, trade unions, debating clubs, and old boys' associations" built upon shared ties to British universities.[12]

Frustration with halting and superficial colonial administrative reforms amid worsening economic conditions soon led to anger and grievances among Nigerians. Young Nigerians were dissatisfied with the indigenous intelligentsia's acceptance of colonial reforms in lieu of full and immediate national independence; many of these young people were persuaded by the anti-colonial rhetoric emanating from the U.S. and the Soviet Union.

Within the British colonial administration, both the Regional and Federal governments stood fast against Marxism-Leninism,[13] enacting laws aimed against radicals, socialists, or leftists of any ilk. Socialism gained ground, however, with the rising tide of militant nationalism.

Leftist ideas were evident both in politics and trade unionism during the period. More important, Nigerian intellectuals and organizers endeavored to adapt communism to their own colonial situation. Hence, as subsequent chapters take up in greater detail, some of them claimed to be Marxists, while others declared themselves Stalinists, Titoists or Maoists. These divisions soon created many pseudo-Marxist organizations in the 1950s and beyond. Nationalism, for its part, became militant partly because of support from the Communist International (from September 1947 Cominform) and its satellites in Europe. Records show, however, that attempts to form a centralized Marxist-Leninist movement in Nigeria in the 1940s and 1950s were both episodic and unorganized.[14] Differences in tactics, combined with volatile personality clashes, spawned uncoordinated and pseudo-Marxist organizations mostly in the southern part of the country.[15]

What emerged was a cluster of pseudo-Marxist groups with different tactics for achieving the shared aim of a Nigerian socialist state that would metamorphose into a Nigerian communist state. Their common ground was reliance upon directives and support from the Communist Party of Great Britain (CPGB) and World Federation of Trade Union (WFTU), although as the evidence shows, such directives were not strictly followed.[16] To some, a mass and nation-wide political party such as the National Council of Nigerian Citizens (NCNC) could serve their purpose (Nduka Eze's group). Others were of the opinion that a Marxist party should be formed so that the bourgeoisie would not hijack the revolution (Samuel Ikoku's group). The latter were of the view that a Marxist party would metamorphose into a Communist Party of Nigeria in the near future. These differences partly explain the absence of a nation-wide Marxist movement and the failure of leftist ideology.

COMMUNISM IN POST-WORLD WAR II NIGERIA

Leftist ideology made in-roads among Nigerian nationalists because it addressed the plight of the working class and the peasantry under colonialism. There is no denying the fact those Nigerian nationalists and labor leaders were generally well informed about leftist ideology. Like their British compatriots,[17] they not only understood the tensions involved in adapting it to their own situation but also ultimately created a distinctive meaning and application of the ideology. They understood the role of the working class and the peasants; the inevitability of the class struggle; the need for contingent co-operation with the bourgeoisie; the aim of the socialist state as a transition to a communist state; and the need for tactical adaptation of the process in relation to their colonial situation. As Lenin himself once declared, "all nations will arrive at socialism . . . but not the same way."[18]

Agunbiade-Bamishe succinctly highlighted the Nigerian situation when he remarked: "I am a Communist on the conviction that a political ideology which is based on the philosophy of Marx-Lenin-Stalinism is the only political ideology that can best serve the interests of the Nigerian people."[19] Samuel Ikoku, in one of his editorials in the *Nigerian Socialist Review* (successor to *Labour Champion,* of which he was a co-editor), exemplified the thinking and goal of the Nigerian Marxists during the 1950s when he wrote that: "We must start a Party . . . the Party of the Working class in alliance with the poor peasantry. It must be guided by the tested theory of the struggles of the working classes the world over—the theory of Marxism-Leninism. It must adopt the road of open and determined revolutionary struggle against imperialism and against all forces of exploitation and oppression."[20]

According to Anglo-American officials (including bourgeois nationalists) Marxist ideas could not be treated lightly. Thus, in Nigeria as elsewhere, preventing the development of leftist ideology and organizations was tied with decolonization and the transfer of power. This book is about the various attempts to develop a nationwide leftist organization in Nigeria between 1945 and 1965, and its consequent failure due partly to official opposition and inability to gain grass root membership.

Chapter Three

Reconstructing the Zikist Movement, 1945–1950

INTRODUCTION

Historically, the infiltration of communist ideology into colonial Africa colonies passed through four stages, each marked by distinctive tactics and goals: First came the propaganda stage when communist literature poured into the country; second, infiltration into labor organizations; third, infiltration into the armed forces; and fourth, a "peace offensive" aimed at the violent overthrow of a government.[1] British analyzes, as in the 1950 official document "A Survey of Communism in Africa," gave a vivid outline of this process and identified Soviet satellites in Europe as the source of the infiltration. British officials were concerned about the activities of "national liberation movements" such as the *"Rassemblement Democratique Africain"* (RDA) in North and West Africa, particularly in the French sector. The Communist Party of South Africa was identified as a potential front in sub-Saharan Africa, especially dangerous to colonial rule if communist activists could exploit racial strife to garner supporters in Kenya and the Rhodesias. Other concerns included 1948 Russian case against colonial powers at the United Nations; the growing influence of Communists in Algeria (on the rise until 1955, when the group was outlawed); Soviet and Chinese aid to neighboring Morocco and Tunisia; and the influence of the French *Confederation General du Travail in North Africa.*[2]

A WEST AFRICAN FOCUS

Of even greater significance were the activities of the communists in neighboring West Africa colonies. It was in French-speaking West Africa that the French Communist Party made its greatest impact in the immediate post-war years. Their efforts bore fruit in the formation of *Group d'Etudes Communistes* in 1943 in Abidjan, Bamako, Bobo-Diolasso, Conakry and Dakar. These Marxists groups organized ideological and training classes for members. It was this group of Africans that formed the *Rassemblement Democratique Africain* (RDA) in 1946 (radical in its orientation at least until after 1955) when member groups known to be allied with radical movements, such as the *Union des Populations du Cameroun* (UPC) were expelled. Under Felix Houphouet-Boigny (later a renegade from the organisation) and Gabriel 'Arbroussier, the RDA aligned with the French Communist Party in Paris at least until 1950.[3] And in French Cameroun, the French were faced with militant activities of the communist-influenced, *Union des Populations du Cameroun* (UPC).[4]

Above all, British officials were also concerned about the *Communist Party of Great Britain's* (CPGB) commitment to encourage and support the formation of a nation-wide Marxist party in British colonies, the possibility of Kremlin exploitation of local discontents, and the long-term aim of the Cominform in gaining some influence.[5]

Studies on nationalism and decolonization in Nigeria have understated the seriousness with which post-World War II British officials viewed growing communist tendencies of a few eloquent nationalists.[6] In fact, colonial administrators had tracked leftist infiltration throughout the interwar era, when young Nigerians were so clearly enamored by communists such as I.T.A. Wallace Johnson and George Padmore, and pan-Africanists such as Du Bois, Marcus Garvey and Ladipo Solanke, and anti-colonialists such as Gandhi and Nehru in India.[7] In these earlier decades, British colonial officials noted with alarm the activities of organizations such as the *Communist Party of Great Britain (CPGB)*, the *International Union of Students (IUS)*, *World Federation of Trade Unions (WFTU)*, the *Women International Democratic Federation (IDF)*, and the *World Federation of Democratic Youth* (WFDY).

While leftist groups drew fine distinctions amongst themselves, to Britain's colonial administrators the landscape of the interwar era was defined by mounting radicalization, as moderate groups lost legitimacy among young Nigerians. Young nationalists and labor unionists grew critical of the seeming inefficacy of associations such as the *National Congress of British West Africa* (1920); *Nigeria National Democratic Party* (1922); the *West African Students Union* (1925); and the *Nigerian Youth Movement* (1934). They were also dissatisfied with British handling of the Italo-Ethiopian crisis (1935); West Indian colonial problems (1935–1938); and the "deep problems of increasing unemployment in urban areas, poverty, social disruptions caused by colonial changes and increasing urbanization, ethnic rivalries, and inadequate schools, as well as the fact that development was in general too slow to meet the aspirations of a population that was becoming better informed."[8]

Immersion in Marxist literature and contacts with the Communist International encouraged radical leftist views; at the same time, British intransigence and these escalating social disruptions convinced activists that militancy was the only meaningful avenue to independence. A few Nigerian youths were also sympathetic to the plight of the Soviets, particularly after the German invasion. Coleman noted that: "earlier in about 1943, Nigerian youths formed the Red Army Club in solidarity with Soviet Russia after the German attack."[9] During the same month "they sent a cable to leaders of Soviet Russia espousing the willingness to establish relations with the youths of Soviet Russia."[10]

Despite superficial similarities between the two processes, Nigeria was an exception to this pattern of leftist in-roads into pseudo-capitalist or colonial societies. Only after World War II did Marxist nationalists and labor unionists emerge as a distinct and powerful voice; still, the number of Communist activists never reached the necessary critical mass and was weakened by sectarianism and generational differences. Many younger Nigerians were looking to Nnamdi Azikiwe to lead the struggle against British rule. As events later showed, though, neither Azikiwe, nor any of the older generation, was prepared for decolonization as a path to communism.

MARXIAN IDEOLOGY AND ZIKISM

According to Awa, Nnamdi Azikiwe was the pioneer leader of Marxian socialism in Nigeria. In 1943, Azikiwe spelled out his theoretical ideas in two booklets: "Economic Reconstruction of Nigeria," and "Political Blueprint of Nigeria." He asserted, "Marxian philosophy with its dynamic analysis should become the basis of a new economic system in the country." He recommended the reorganization of the economic and political systems to usher in socialism, with the proviso that such reorganization should be done through the democratic process.[11] Ultimately, however, Azikiwe abandoned socialism for free trade, constitutionalism and moral re-armament. One can speculate three reasons for his change of heart: the assassination story of 1945, his membership of Moral Re-armament Group in 1949 and the reality of the colonial situation.[12] He nonetheless provided the lead in ideological orientation in nationalist politics.

Azikiwe stated that the aftermath of the General Strike of 1945 was "the emergence of ideological movements whose objectives included not only political freedom, but also social equality and economic security."[13]

Nigerian youth provided the leadership in "practical" ideological move-ments. The youth were tired of "long articles, plenty of talks and no work" that had become the feature of elite nationalism up to 1945.[14] In fact, with the collapse of the *Nigerian Youth Movement* and the formation of the *National Council for Nigeria and the Cameroons* (later, National Council of Nigerian Citizens) in August 1944, some Nigerian youths felt that there was need to start a socialist movement.[15]

Earlier in 1945, Amanke Okafor formed a Marxist group called "Talakawa Party." It did not, however, exist as a political party but as a think-tank group. Its aim was to rally the working class together in order to "achieve a free independent and a socialist Nigeria." This group however made no real impact because its founder/leader soon left Nigeria for further studies in the United Kingdom, where he joined the Communist Party of Great Britain and was featured in its activities before his return to Nigeria in early 1950s.[16]

On July 8, 1945, the *Nigerian National Socialist Party* was born under the leadership of Fola Arogundade. Other members were A. Chuk-wura, Babatunde Shotade, G. Menkiti, Mudashiru Dawodu, Shola Morris, S. Okeke, Alli Zazau and Alabi McIver.[17] Its secretariat was located at 9 Ondo Street, Ebute-Metta East, Lagos. This embryonic organization did not enjoy the support of older nationalists because of its communist orien-tation.[18] Members regarded capitalism as the cause of Nigerian misery. According to them, "it had encouraged the enactment of inhuman legisla-tion to foster the degeneration of mankind."[19] Despite anti-capitalist rheto-ric, the leader of the *NNSP* lamented after its collapse "its adherents were a very meek and weak lot of young people . . . We want to practice socialism but we are an ignorant mass of citizens comforted by the maxim that none can learn to swim until one is in the water."[20] The organization was a non-starter and its immediate collapse was not surprising. Its leader's remark is but a reflection on why many would-be leftist organizations during the colonial era did not long endure.

Between 1946 when the *Zikist Movement* was formed and 1948 when it assumed a militant posture towards the British administration in Nigeria, the stage seemed set for Nigerian Marxists and their sympathizers in the struggle against British colonialism. On February 16, 1946, young radical Nigerians within the *NCNC* formed a movement, which derived its inspiration from Nnamdi Azikiwe himself. Its founding members were Kola Balogun (first President), C.K. Ajuluchukwu (the first secretary-gen-eral), Andrew Agams, Abiodun Aloba and Nduka Eze. Other members included Raji Abdallah (second President), Osita Agwuna, K.O. Mbadiwe, Ogedengbe Macaulay, Ikenna Nzimiro, Mokwugo Okoye and Ralph

Aniedobe.[21] It should be stressed here that contrary to official perception that the Zikist Movement was full of "irresponsible young men,"[22] the formation of the Movement was due to their growing impatience with what they considered to be the slow pace of Nigeria's political advancement during the period.[1]

The Zikist Movement was formed in order to espouse and perpetuate Zikism as a resplendent universal philosophy. At its formation local colonial reality was the dictating factor rather than international idealism. Leftist ideology was however the philosophical energizer in their struggle against the anachronistic British rules. Hence they did not rule out violence against the British in Nigeria. This view however was soon overwhelmed (as will be shown later) by pacifism—a philosophy that recognizes compromise.

By October 1948, Osita Agwuna had made his "A Call for Revolution," where he called for a peace offensive against the British administration in Nigeria. In February 1949, Ogedengbe Macaulay talked of "dragging of the government down, and seizing power by force."[2] During the same month, Raji Abdallah implored his northern brethren to join in the violent struggle.[3] He also called for "positive action to end British rule" (this phrase was later used by the Convention Peoples Party (*CPP*) of the Gold Coast).[4] Although government clamped down on them by arresting and charging ten of them with sedition in 1949,[5] this did not deter other members from inciting other uprisings in other parts of the country.

Azikiwe used the N.C.N.C Convention of April 1949 in Lagos to call for moderation and discipline among his followers, particularly the Zikists. He denounced militancy and revolution and called on all militant elements to ponder deeply the reasonableness and viability of a positive action without a mobilized force, a disciplined army, a well-protected general staff, a line of communication, and lastly a cause worth fighting and dying for.

This view generated many comments from Zikist leadership. On April 6, 1949, a commentary published in *African Echo* denounced Azikiwe's view as "a disappointing and distracting declaration." The commentary concluded that, "For our part, we wonder where Zik will get any army to mobilize when the time comes. Certainly, not those disappointed and disillusioned disciples of Zikism would again freely offer their services."[6]

On February 16, 1950, the colonial police Special Branch uncovered Zikist sabotage plan after several raids that cut across the nation. In the Northern Provinces, fifteen persons' houses were searched and seditious documents were found in eleven of them. They were all prosecuted and found guilty by the colonial magistrate courts. In the Eastern provinces, seven houses were searched and two persons in Onitsha and Enugu were arrested and charged for like offences. The search and arrest of Ikenna

Nzimiro's house at Onitsha (he was the secretary of the Onitsha Branch of the Movement) drew much excitement. The document entitled "The National Programme" was found in the house of Nzimiro at Onitsha. The document was in code, the key to which was also found. The document and code was for the use of Zikist Movement members, the N.N.F.L. and the U.A.C. Amalgamated Workers Union, the three bodies with which Nduka Eze was intimately associated. Other documents found included plans to destroy oil storage centers and essential government houses. During the prosecution, Nzimiro confirmed receiving the messages in his mailbox on February 7, 1950, and was awaiting further instructions before the police search. He was found guilty of sedition and sentenced to nine months in prison.[7]

The height of Zikist activities was an abortive attempt on the life of Chief Secretary Hugh Foot in early 1950.[8] On February 18, 1950, *Reuters* reported that a young Ibo man named Heelas Chukwuma Ugokwe, of the Posts and Telegraph Department, attacked Foot with a knife when the Chief Secretary was entering the Secretariat building in Lagos. Two days later, Ugokwe was charged with attempted murder; on March 13, 1950, Mr. Justice Rhodes at the Lagos Magistrate Court sentenced Ugokwe to life imprisonment.[9]

In his report to the Secretary of State, Governor Macpherson laid full blame for the assassination plan on the Zikist Movement, noting that Ugokwe, a World War II veteran, had joined the Zikist Movement at its inception in 1946.[10] He, along with eleven other youths, was allegedly specifically recruited as an "assassin" during the Zikist Movement convention at Kaduna in December of 1949 to carry out a nation-wide plot aimed at the forcible seizure of power from the government.[11] It was further claimed that Mokwugo Okoye personally issued instructions for this assignment.[12] Initially, Ugokwe's target was Macpherson himself, but after waiting nine days without finding an opportunity to kill the Governor (Secretary of State for colonies); he shifted his sights to the Chief Secretary. Fellow Zikists and their sympathizers applauded Ugokwe's action. Ndolue, on behalf of others, directed an appeal to the West African Court of Appeal, which reduced Ugokwe's life sentence to a twelve-year prison term.[13]

This incident predictably led to a tightening of security within official circles, and the eventual banning of the movement under the "Unlawful Societies Act, April 1950." A public notice in mid-April, 1950, declared "conclusive evidence has been obtained from many parts of the country that the Zikist Movement is an organization, which aims to stir up hatred and malice and to pursue seditious aims, by lawlessness and violence."[14] The government also confiscated "all banners, insignia arms, papers, books, documents and any similar property" of the organization.[15]

ZIKISM AS ANTI-COLONIAL LEFTISM

The philosophy of the Zikist Movement was largely nationalistic with a strong admixture of Communist Party terminology, the adoption of a Marxist philosophy and a complete opposition to colonial government in any form. The Movement was revolutionary and considered the colonial tutelage an anathema to the development of the people of Nigeria.

Although the Zikist Movement was banned in April of 1950, this did not extirpate it entirely. It survived through a re-grouping of interests and tactics. This tactical shift was two fold. First, the older generation was eliminated as active participants and leaders in the Movement, in large part because Azikiwe and others in his cohort abandoned the Zikists' course. With the generational shift, reformism and military action now took second seat behind an organizational putsch that "aimed to maneuver their opponents (Nigerians and British) in debates, elections and practical work." As Okoye succinctly puts it: "The point here is to beat the opponent at his own game by demonstrating a superior intellect, energy and patriotism, thus throwing doubt in the enemy's mind as to the value of his ideals or lack of them while at the same time showing that the methods and aims of the revolutionary group are preferable to any other." This "organisational putschism" is to be distinguished from sheer reformism or Fabianism which is essentially a doctrine of middle class complacence and only thrives where national prosperity is high and there are no sharp distinctions between classes." Various branches of the Zikist Movement tabled resolutions counseling violence to members. An extract from one by the Onitsha branch being typical of the whole:

(1) Gymnastic exercises—All Branch Committees shall learn: Forest escapades and studies; Fasting in the Camping; Swimming; Military Tactics.

(2) Arrests of Members—On the pronouncement of sentences: The magistrate or Judge shall be dealt with; The Incendiary explosive shall be laid if possible under the seat of the Judge or magistrate around the courts."[16]

Second, the flow of communist literature into the country through the CPGB in London grew in volume, reaching Zikists and other communist or socialist followers. To illustrate, in November of 1950, out of a total of seventy sacks of second-class mail, six were taken at random and examined; in each sack examined, there were 1,000 communist pamphlets, and it was estimated that 50,000 pamphlets must have entered Nigeria by one mail boat alone.[17] In the latter half of 1952 and the beginning of 1953, the volume perceptibility increased and at the same time there was a change in emphasis. Earlier types of propaganda were Marxist books, propaganda acclaiming the Russian way of life and Stalin's virtues. These types were quickly overtaken by Cold War propaganda, anti-colonial propaganda, and newspapers and periodicals critiques. There were an increased number of pamphlets sent to private addresses despite the fact that the people could not pay for them.[18]

While the Zikist motto was "secrecy and ruthless execution of our plans,"[19] the movement confusingly vacillated between pro- and anti-British statements, responding in large part to anti-leftist British colonial initiatives. After 1950, the leftist orientation was much clearer, and membership of the organization was insistently colored by Marxian teachings.[20] Zikism invoked a vague vision of African irredentism, an idea drawn from Azikiwe's *Renascent Africa* (1937).

The Movement had nine goals, spelled out thus:

(1) To study painstakingly and objectively, practice conscientiously, seriously and constitutionally the creed of "Zikism" as set out by Dr. Nnamdi Azikiwe in his Renascent Africa and allied teachings and as propounded in its philosophical form by Nwafor Orizu;"

(2) "To faithfully follow the leadership of Dr. Azikiwe;"

(3) "To courageously and intelligently preach Zikism, making it understandable to the mass of the indigenous elements of the country with the purpose of aiding the evolution of a united nation out of the varied tribes of Nigeria and the British Cameroons;"

(4) "To faithfully dedicate our lives to the task of African Redemption by concretely demonstrating and defending even at the risk of paying the supreme sacrifice, the Zikist way of life;"

(5) "To use every available means of submitting constitutionally the opinions, feelings, sentiments and customs of the people of the country to the British Government of Nigeria;"

(6) "To take interest in all activities, events, happenings and practices that affects the destiny of this country'"

(7) "To co-operate with other organisations in the country whose aims and aspirations do not clash with those of this movement;"

(8) "To co-operate with the Zikist Movement the world over;" and,

(9) "To raise funds from Zikists and the general public in furtherance of these objects."[21]

In fact, British and American officials were justifiably apprehensive about the implications of these tenets. The Marxian vision inspiring the creed was suggested in a Zikist-sponsored editorial on September 3, 1946, in *Nigerian Spokesman,* castigating the Police Force, the Army, and lawyers. As to the last, for example, the editorial declared that: "a lawyer becomes a societal flower and even an anachronism in the United Nigeria Republic since his profession is based on laws enacted by the former (colonial) rulers." The editorial continued, "The Army and the Police Force would have to be disbanded and reformed because they are co-operative part of what socialists recognize as the state machine."[22]

Apart from sponsored editorials in *African Echo, Nigerian Spokesman, Daily Comet* and the *West African Pilot* (before 1949), the Zikists aired their agenda in the "Zimo Newsletter," the official publication of the organization. In addition to exegeses on Marxist-Leninist thought and philosophy, topics included, "What is the Zikist Movement?" and "Workers of Nigeria Revolt." The Zikists openly declared their commitment to socialism and explicitly endorsed the Marxist thesis that economic factors conditioned the moral, legal and political aspects in the development of any given society.[23]

This explains why members of the Zikist Movement were variously described as a "Communist propagandist," and a "band of youths who advocated the violent overthrow of the British administration." Some of them (i.e. Abdallah and Oged Macaulay) were described as making "violently anti-Government speeches in public," contrary to their employment in the colonial civil service. Osita Agwuna, author of "A Call for Revolution," was described as a man "inclined increasingly towards violence . . . probably because he aspires to make a martyr of himself."[24]

Perhaps British officials were right to fear for themselves and the colonial regime. As early as October 9, 1948, Agwuna issued a call to 'positive action' at a meeting of the Lagos branch of the NCNC at the Yaba Stadium; he proposed a resolution accusing the government of fanning tribal discord by encouraging "minority elements."[25] He then called upon those present to pledge "to take any measure to silence the 'minority' and to overthrow the Government and handover power to the NCNC."[26] As the report shows, wiser counsels at the meeting prevailed, and the resolution was withdrawn.

However, in late October—just three weeks later—Agwuna followed up with "A Call for Revolution." In that lecture, he identified Nigeria's two principal enemies: the first was the Government itself, and the second was the people's fearful reluctance to rise up and drive out that Government. As far as he was concerned, the only hope of salvation was progressive revolution beginning with a civil disobedience campaign. He then recommended that every taxable Nigerian refuse to pay taxes to the Government but remit an equivalent amount into the *NCNC* coffers. In addition, Empire Day should stop forthwith; nobody should join the civil service or the army; and the *NCNC* on its forthcoming tour should "preach a doctrine of hate and contempt for the Government."[27]

ZIKISM AS A CALL TO ACTION

Agwuna's "A Call for Revolution" is worth reproducing in full, as it well illustrates his Marxist foundations and temperament:

"A CALL FOR REVOLUTION"

(a) "Like heroes let us show the spirit to dare and conquer; let us forget the momentary interests of our cumbrous flesh and pursue a lasting pearl that is freedom; let us fight for the honour of smashing the present Imperialist State machine BY AS FOUL AND VICIOUS METHODS AS WITH WHICH WE ARE STILL CAPTIVATED; let us for once cast aside that simplicity and complacency which have been a curse to our race and cultivate those wordy virtues which speak, use and understand the language of the World in every changing epoch;"

(b) "Our youth must then assimilate the methods of India, Burma, Indonesia, Lybia (sic) and Palestine, where unwilling Rulers have been shown their way out; MUST DAMN RELIGIOUS AND HUMANIST INHIBITIONS and, where the means is certain of the end, work on the hypothesis that the end justifies the means. MUST EMBRACE ACTIVE REVOLUTION AS THE CURRENT WORLD ORDER, MUST EMBRACE THE SCIENTIFIC USE OF FORCE for justice without force, it is said, is powerless; and force without justice is tyranny."

(c) "The youths of Africa should interest themselves in Military tactics of defence, in physical adventures of all kinds and should demonstrate more than a passing and academic interest in the methods and tactics of revolutionary movements in other countries and seek communion with them. In particular, they should organize themselves for intensified picketing and boycott. DELIBERATE GROUP VIOLATION OF EVERY LAW and executive order which they deem to be tyrannical and a breach of human right and for various forms of revolutionary activities and should highly resolve to save this continent from the predatory clutches of Imperialism through any mean."[28]

Agwuna's Marxian call to action led to the arrest of the meeting's chairman, Anthony Enahoro, together with Duke Dafe and Ralph Aniedobe, and their prosecution for sedition at the colonial court. Although the arrests did not occasion much excitement initially, some of the ex-servicemen soon came out with attacks on Azikiwe saying that "he put these young men up to making the speech and that if he was the patriot he held himself to be he would have insisted on going to prison with them."[29]

The prosecution of these men notwithstanding, other Zikists continued the struggle. In mid-November of 1948, an unsigned message was issued from the Zikist Movement secretariat in Lagos and distributed throughout the country.

The message read thus:

NATIONALIST MESSAGE LAGOS

"Be it known by all Zikists and freedom-loving Nigerians that this is the hour. The Zikist Movement can no longer hope to have reason where, it is evident; respect for reason does not exist. The movement is therefore calling upon the youths of the country to support it in the present struggle for freedom. We cannot allow this challenge to our manhood to go. The Zikist Movement, in humble obedience to the call, is now ordering all the branches and regional presidents to organize and lead campaigns throughout the country so as to makes our stand known. Our branches and branch officers should not antagonize any tribal and political groups. The campaign should aim at focusing the attention of the masses towards the one common central danger—the British Government."[30]

While the Azikiwe-led *NCNC* seemed ambivalent, Abdallah and other Zikists opted to identify themselves completely with Agwuna on the need for a "positive action." The Zikists lost no time in trying to whip up excitement both in Lagos and in the provinces. In late November 1948, a seven-point instruction was passed on to branches outside Lagos for implementation. These were:

(I)   "A campaign should be held by summoning meetings with executives of private unions, family unions, headmasters, explaining to them the need for progressive revolution beginning with civil disobedience without violence or non-cooperation;"

(II)   "If our men now standing trial are sentenced without option of fine, the workers and market women should make positive demands to government to release them. Such demands should be followed up with an ultimatum, organised slow strike and stop marketing;"

(III)   "In the event of the government contravening such ultimatum, a country-wide demonstration should follow by damaging mercantile houses, prison walls, post offices, police barracks and police rifles should be seized first; time limit for all these will be December 24th 1948;"

(IV)   "Our order to all branches should read as follows: "I believe in genuine and beneficial co-operation—ZAKARI;"

(V)   "On receipt of this instruction, summon all regional presidents and secretaries and distribute these instructions to them";

(VI)   "From now onwards all private and important documents should be dispatched to the headquarters only by sending a messenger by land;" and,

(VII   "Our struggle for freedom does not consist only in pouring abuse, what we need to do is to wage war on those forces against us."[31]

These instructions led to the mobilization of groups to disrupt the preliminary proceedings in the sedition cases against the Zikists in Lagos as well as a demonstration in Onitsha that prompted the closure of the market for one day.[32] On this occasion, Abdallah and Oged Macaulay were arrested, leaving Eze, Okoye, Ndulue and others to continue with the struggle. On September 5, 1949, the Zikist Movement, under the temporary leadership of Eze and Okoye, issued an operation order to its members to organize "a peasant movement throughout the country."[33]

In addition, members were implored to infiltrate trade unions and seek positions within those organizations to prepare the way for later civil disobedience demonstrations.[34] Young people were also encouraged to "embrace active revolution and deliberate group violation of every law and executive order."[35] That Marxist-Leninist tenets and the vision of a Nigerian Communist State inspired this operational order is clear in its call for active revolution and for the re-awakening of the peasantry and proletariat.

In late February of 1950, Nigerian police and Special Branch agents raided the Zikist Movement's headquarters, arresting sixteen people. Three were discharged, one was fined £25, ten were sentenced to six-month imprisonment, and two others were given terms of two to four weeks.[36]

Mokwugo Okoye, the secretary-general of the Zikist Movement, received the harshest sentence: a prison term of thirty-three months for possessing seditious documents. Hence, when others regained their freedom, he was still serving his sentence despite Ndulue's solicitation of the British Labour Party members of parliament, Fenner Brockway and Reginald Sorenson, to lobby for a Royal pardon.[37]

Brockway's appeal to the Secretary of State for the Colonies was turned down because in the first instance the Governor and not the Secretary of State exercised the Royal Prerogative for the Colonies. The Secretary of State for the Colonies only intervened if there was evidence of a failure of due process in the colonial courts. A Colonial Office official noted that "the circumstances of the case do not justify his own intervention in a matter in which the Governor is in the best position to judge the desirability or otherwise of exercising his powers."[38]

The Colonial Office was therefore right to have concluded, "It was not only wrong for Brockway to send an appeal directly to London, the Zikists were engaged in a plot and not a riot, and as such the invocation of liberalism to permit the release of those found guilty of plotting violence is a trifle inappropriate."[39]

While Chapter Six addresses United States reactions to the leftists' problem, it is important to stress now those Anglo-American anxieties about the mix of communism and Zikists' activities were not limited to known nationalist groups. Intelligence reports confirmed that nationalist organizations had abetted the Marxist penetration of student groups and labor unions as well. In Lagos, American diplomats and British administrators were concerned about growing radical tendencies within the University College, Ibadan. As Erwin Keeler noted in a dispatch to the State Department in Washington D.C. "The intensely political and radical atmosphere of the campus is already established, with the encouragement and direct assistance by the local nationalist leaders."[40]

As evidence that nationalist leaders had targeted the College, Keeler recalled the remarks of Kingsley Mbadiwe, an *NCNC* leader, during the 1952 budget session of the Nigerian House of Representatives.[41] During the discussion of government financial support of the College, Mbadiwe stated that, "If money was to be spent upon the College it should and must be made a place where young Nigerians were trained to be nationalists."[42] Such statements convinced Keeler that Nigerian students made "a prime target of the communists at such future time as the opportunity might become auspicious for them."[43] As Chapters Three through Eight shows, it was the direction of things in the labor unions that provoked the most vociferous official anxiety.

There were some Nigerians who believed in the assurance of independence within a reasonable period. They were not interested in whether it is linked with any political or economic thought. What was important to them is independence from the colonial power. Mbonu Ojike, Area Council/NNDP member of the Lagos Town Council aptly represent this school of thought when he writes inter alia in *The Road to Freedom* that;

> "We should not be afraid if the economy is linked to any form of -ism. All he needs is GROWTH. Capitalism, socialism, or communism, which ever answers his call most effectively, let him pursue it unafraid of name-calling propaganda. Let him follow any economic road that most quickly leads towards freedom to transact business in his own country and with the outer world."[44]

CONCLUSION

This chapter has traced the process by which Marxian ideology gained prominence in the Zikist movement. To the young people, the realization of a Marxian vision through the NCNC would have been feasible but for Azikiwe's ideological re-orientation and complacency for a Marxian pathway to independence. Understandably, Marxists pursued their own ideological strategy, endeavoring to develop a nation-wide Marxist group separate and apart from the existing nationalist group. The next chapter discusses these efforts during the 1950s.

Chapter Four

Marxism During the 1950s: Reformation, Regrouping, and the Future

INTRODUCTION

The banning of the Zikist Movement did not lead to the extirpation of Marxian ideology in Nigeria, and most certainly did not discourage attempts to build Marxist organizations. Still, the assault on Zikism prompted activists to shift their energies away from a nation-wide organization and instead devote themselves to building strong local groups. These efforts produced many embryonic Marxist organizations in Nigeria in the 1950s, although the Nigerian working class movement remained separate and apart, as it had been through the 1940s. The Communist Party of Great Britain, the main satellite with which Nigerian Marxists were closely associated, was perturbed about the eruption of Marxist splinter groups, formed and re-formed throughout the late 1950s.

NIGERIANS AND THE PRESSURE FOR PROGRESS

There was pressure both inside and outside Nigeria, as elsewhere in the colonies for colonial reforms and development after World War II. Understanding the situation during this period would shed light into the role of the Marxist and other leftist organizations during the 1950s. Leftist organizations generally did not trust colonial administrators in terms of their claims to develop the economy and social structure. To them the goal of the colonial state was to consolidate its hegemony by all means, police and sanction the leftist groups, and ensure the integration of colonial economy into the capitalist world. Constitutional development, socio-economic development plans and inclusion of conservative nationalist leaders in administration were seen as camouflage and deceptive measures aimed at dividing the leftist group.

It seems there was an "imperial responsibility" on paper rather than in action as Nigerian Marxists, like their counterparts in the Gold Coast, British and French Cameroon, gained momentum and regrouped to challenge the colonial administration and leading nationalist parties participating in the devolution program. There was a broad-based demand for reforms in view of the poverty among the majority of the people—farmers, small business owners, market women, government workers, and the whole citizenry, for a redistribution of the nations' wealth. What distinguished leftist groups from mainstream nationalist groups was the road towards achieving reforms and wealth redistribution among the people.

For instance when in late 1949, John Macpherson (new colonial governor general) instituted a nationwide debate to review and revise the Richard's constitution of 1946, the leftists were not satisfied with the process. The Richard constitution had been criticized partly because of its regionalism, non-consultation with Nigerians, divide-and-rule tactics, and ethnic division. Although Macpherson allowed and encouraged participation by Nigerians in what later became Macpherson constitution in 1951, the leftists saw the process as anti "pan-Nigerianism." The idea of collectivity, people's power, and socialism remained elusive. What obtained was the perpetuation of regionalism and sectionalism, quasi-federalism, and continued disparity between the poor and the rich.

Anti-colonial feelings were not however limited to internal events. Nigerians were not insulated from the growing Pan-African ferment, Ethiopian defeat of Italy, the series of riots in British West Indies colonies between 1935 and 1938, and criticism by leading British scholars, organizations, and administrators. The role and writings of such eminent people such as Richard Coupland, Lord Hailey, Margery Perham, William Macmillan, and William McLean is too well known to be retold here. It seems however that the most influential effort was from the British Fabian Colonial Bureau. The Bureau with its constant anti-colonial views and its members' role within the British House of Parliament influenced Nigerian Marxists in challenging colonial rule and the call for freedom.

It was in this environment that the leftists committed to keeping the pressure on British colonial rule to reform and give political freedom. Since they were marginalized in the mainstream nationalist political parties, they formed groups in the fifties that promoted ideological alternatives to colonial socio-political, economic, and cultural reforms through debates, newspaper publications, and protests as occasion permitted.

MARXIST GROUPS IN THE 1950S

The Communist Party of Great Britain (CPGB) identified at least six differ-ent groups of Nigerian Marxist organizations operating in 1953, while also conceding that there may have been groups on which it had no facts.[1] In November 1950, Nduka Eze, undoubtedly the most outstanding defender of the Nigerian working class, had formed the Freedom Movement as a vehicle for the crusade to liberate Nigeria and Nigerians. The Freedom Movement aspired to replace the banned Zikist Movement and continue the struggle for Nigeria's independence under communist auspices. It organized Marxist lectures and discussions and circulated Marxist litera-ture on different subjects.[2] By October of 1951, however, ideological con-flicts and stiff government opposition had rendered the group defunct.

Earlier in 1951, another group had emerged in Ibadan called "The Communist Party of Nigeria and the Cameroons." The only record of the organization is a letter sent to the CPGB office (London) from Ibadan on March 19, 1951, by Samuel Alamu and O.O. Gbolahan. A membership roster is not available, nor is a record of their activities, as is the case with most Nigerian Marxist groups during the period. This group was likely a clique of young people interested in obtaining assistance from the CPGB and the *Daily Worker* for membership education efforts.[3] The organization was a Communist Party in name only and had no discernable impact on the contemporary political scene; remnants later became associated with the "Lagos Marxist" which established The League in February of 1951.

Formed as a result of the momentary fusion of two existing Marxist groups in Lagos (Eze and Ikoku/Ogunsheye factions), The League emerged to "initiate, direct and guide the building of a many-sided and nation-wide working class movement on the basis of Marxism."[4] This was the first time, and perhaps the last, when the Marxists were united. By early 1952, Ikoku/Ogunsheye group had formed another group called the Committee for People's Independence, renamed the Peoples Committee for Indepen-dence, in February of 1952.

Even during its short time span, The League had considerable impact among Nigerian Marxists. Formed by eighteen comrades, The League's activities were threefold: (a) "To disseminate Marxist thought throughout the country;" (b) "To initiate purely Marxist ideas through trade unions, political and other organisations;" and (c) "To formulate policies for the individual of the Marxist organisations (i.e. trade unions, political parties, peasants, youths, women, student and ex-servicemen's organisations)."[5] At their weekly meetings on the ideological education of members, discussion leaders focused on one or another particular aspect of Marxism then led a general discussion on a topic of the day in order to move comrades from the abstract and theoretical to the realm of action and implementation.

Over time, when leaders found that justice could not be done to the study of Marxism in these ordinary meetings, they arranged a series of special, mostly secret, meetings to cover both local and international issues, including (a) "Marxism as a scientific approach to the study of human society;" (b) "Social development and the laws that govern it;" (c) "The nature of capitalist society;" (d) "Imperialism;" (e) "The post-war tactics of imperialism;" (f) "Marxist tactics (general—in the trade unions, reactionary parliaments, compromise, etc);" (g) "The dangers of overseas capital with special reference to Nigerian Government policy;" (h) "The Persian oil dispute;" (i) "The local political scene (from time to time);" and, (j) "The constitution."[6]

While it is difficult to evaluate the success of these programs, at least in terms of intention and indoctrination, they did mark an improvement in Marxists' efforts to influence the political modernization of the colonial state during the 1950s. By early 1953, however, The League had died, primarily because of personality clashes amongst its leaders. Those who left (Agwuna, Ogunsheye, Nzimiro, Ikoku, etc) formed the Peoples Committee for Independence, discussed more fully below.

A group calling itself the Nigeria Convention Peoples Party formed in 1951, a few months after creation of The League. This was not a political party, but yet one more splinter Marxist group formed by Eze's former followers. One of its leading members was Ikoro, a former close associate of Eze. This group was more inclined towards the Gold Coast CPP and made fruitless efforts to garner financial support from it.[7] As in the case of previously organized groups, one of the main reasons for its formation was the personality clash among Nigerian Marxists precipitated by the failure of the December 1950 labor strike. The group nonetheless preached "scientific socialism to the masses in the village, workers in the factory, unemployed ex-servicemen, youths, and progressive intellectuals."[8] With inspiration from Palme Dutt's "Britain's Crisis of the Empire," its leader (Ikoro) published a pamphlet entitled "Imperialism versus the People," castigating British rule in Nigeria, and warning Nigerian Marxists that theory alone would not bring socialism to Africans.[9] Interestingly, unlike other groups, the Nigeria CPP openly stated its willingness to accept directives from the CPGB concerning it activities in Nigeria.[10]

Perhaps the most formidable group emerging from Eze's debacle was the Peoples Committee for Independence, formed in February of 1952. With its office in the Lagos suburb of Yaba, the new group's declared ultimate objective was to build a mass and united nationalist movement, seize power, and establish a socialist society. This involved "waging an uncompromising battle against British imperialism and the reactionary forces within the ranks of our countrymen."[11] For them, Marxism was a guide to action, embodied and enriched by the experiences of common people all over the world struggling for national independence. Thus, Marxism was "open to adaptation and should not be seen as a set of ready-made rules."[12] As had previous groups, they identified ideological education, the use of trade unions, and the pursuit of unity as absolutely vital to success.

At a meeting on May 7, 1952, executive members of the Peoples Committee for Independence (Ikoku, Ogunsheye, Gogo Nzeribe, D. Fatogun, J. Onwugbuzie) took a dramatic political stride, agreeing to form a nation-wide Marxist-Leninist political party that would unify all existing pseudo-Marxist groups.[13]

This initiative went aground, falling short of CPGB expectations, when Marxist sects attacked Ikoku and the others for posing as saviors and saints. Some members of the Peoples Committee for Independence were also involved in the formation of another group in July of 1952, the United Working Peoples Party. Its first secretary was Ogunsheye, who was then replaced by Uche Omo, upon the former's late 1952 appointment in the Labour Department.[14] It comprised some "returnees," most notably Anozie, Anagbogu, and Onwugbuzie. This group distanced themselves from the main political parties, maintaining that the dominant position of the bourgeoisie in those parties thwarted the progress of communism and foreclosed socialist solutions.[15]

In the absence of adequate information (even from the CPGB and British TUC archives) it is difficult to assess the strength and influence of the U.W.P.P. It is, however, clear that the group was confined to the Eastern Region. By 1955, they had modified their anti-party position and were openly working in alliance with the Action Group and the U.N.I.P. (Chike Obi's party, a break-away from the N.C.N.C.).[16] In September 1955, the U.W.P.P. and U.N.I.P. made futile attempts to disrupt activities of the Azikiwe-led N.C.N.C. government in the Eastern Region. A joint statement calling for an army to fight "the combined forms of imperialism and reactionary leadership of the N.C.N.C." was issued in Enugu.[17] There is no indication that the Action Group was involved in this.[18] When most of its leading members joined the main political parties or took employment in government departments, the U.W.P.P. died naturally before the end of 1955.

IKOKU AND THE NIGERIAN SOCIALIST REVIEW

Among the most prolific Marxists during the 1950s was Samuel Ikoku, initially one of Eze's followers. With others, Ikoku broke away, and in 1952 formed the Peoples Committee for Independence and, later that same year, the United Working Peoples Party. In his various correspondences with CPGB and WFTU leaders, he emphasized the need for a sustainable press for the propagation of Marxist ideas.[19] Ikoku had been joint editor of the *Labour Champion*, established in 1950, and he blamed the collapse of the journal on Eze and Ezumah.

In early February, with support from CPGB and the WFTU, Ikoku began publishing another newspaper, the *Nigerian Socialist Review*.[20] Although the *Review* suffered the fate of its predecessor after a government clamp down on its editor in late 1952, Ikoku articulated several important ideological and tactical ideas. In the inaugural edition (29 February 1952), Ikoku called for a new party of the working class in combination with Marxist intellectuals and the impoverished peasantry.[21] Defying Eze's view that Marxists should work within existing political parties, the editorial asserted that this "new party" should "be the rallying centre of all the finest elements in the working class, who have direct connections with the non-Party organisations of the working class and frequently lead them."[22] This latter category of non-party organizations referred to the U.W.P.P. and P.C.I., both Marxist groups of which he was a member.

This new party was to be guided strictly by Marxist-Leninist theory. Leaders should "adopt the road of open and determined revolutionary struggle against imperialism and against all forces of exploitation and oppression. It must be an efficient and virile organisation on a national scale."[23] There is no doubting the fact that Ikoku and other members of the editorial board (C.O. Mmaba and Meke Anagbogu) were Stalinists. Their position as shown in the various publications before government crackdown on them in late 1952 and early 1953 was strictly Stalinist, and indeed that "there is no alternative to Stalinism in the Marx-Lenin tradition."[24] Emphasizing the need for a working class party, Ikoku quoted Stalin to justify his position that "Its function is to combine the work of all the mass organisations of the proletariat (i.e. the working class) without exception and to direct their activities toward a single goal, the goal of the emancipation of the proletariat."[25]

This was the first stage in the struggle, to use the new party to make Marxists truly independent of the bourgeoisie. During the supposed second stage, a National Front would be formed to act as the army of the revolution.[26] Successful completion of this stage and the defeat of British imperialism, Ikoku predicted, would usher in the third stage—completion of the democratic revolution (the fight for the security and guarantee of political rights for all).[27]

Marxists' vision in Nigeria included acquiring political power and concentrating it in the hands of the "toiling masses." These were seen as the culminating stage towards Marxist "revolution" in Nigeria. Ikoku maintained that "this is the road for us to tread, this is our line of match." He concluded, like a true Stalinist that, "it is the only sure road to national independence and working class emancipation." Assurance of a victory, however, absolutely required this "new party."[28] In a short article entitled *"A Young Socialist at Work,"* C.O. Mmaba supported this vision, reiterating the need for unity among Marxist intellectuals as a prelude to a successful inauguration of a working people's party encompassing all existing Marxist groups.[29]

In the second edition of *Nigerian Socialist Review,* published on March 14, 1952, Ikoku concentrated upon the workers themselves. He argued that the workers themselves could only achieve the emancipation of the working class by organizing independent parties, associations, and trade unions in order to propagate and realize the ideas of Communism.[30] It was in support of this position that Meke Anagbogu asserted in his "Unfurling the banner of Struggle for Independence and Socialism," that "only a revolutionary mass movement, headed by the working class and its political party, can effectively and sincerely fight for independence and socialism not for reforms and capitalism."[31] Predictably, the Nigerian Socialist Review was outlawed in January 1953, under the "Unlawful Publication Ordinance 1950." Its editor was later jailed for sedition and unlawful possession of some copies.[32]

THE INTERNATIONAL DEPARTMENT AND NIGERIAN MARXISTS

The International Department of the CPGB was responsible for molding and guiding ideological orientation of members and fraternities in the colonies. During the 1950s, CPGB officials, including Palme Dutt, Cox, Harry Pollitt, and Barbara Rehumen, were more concerned about the internal conflict among Nigerian Marxists because it prevented the creation of a nationwide organization. Efforts toward resolving the conflict invariably brought direct CPGB intervention in Nigerian affairs. In devising their approach, CPGB officials resisted the impulse to choose between rival Marxist groups. Experience had shown that when individual Nigerians had returned from England and Europe claiming to have the backing of the European and/or British communists, this only exacerbated existing tensions, widening the divisions among Nigerian Marxists.

This had been the result when, for example, Anagbogu returned to Nigeria in December 1952, claiming to have secured pledges of "fraternal assistance from abroad," and Aggams similar assertion that he had official

CPGB backing.[33] In the face of these divisive claims, it became necessary for Harry Pollitt to issue a letter making it clear that no one returning to Nigeria had any authority to speak for the CPGB.[34] As well, from the early 1950s on, the International Department refrained from any official contact, even by post. The rule of secrecy was predicated on making official letters unofficial. Letters from London to Lagos were sent as personal letters rather than official.[35]

The CPGB International Department thus urged conflicting Nigerian Marxist groups to come together, thrash out their differences, and formulate a consensus-based policy and program.[36] This is not to say that the CPGB did not have its own view about the most promising "road to a Marxist Party" in Nigeria. They evidently supported Eze's vision, observing that, "a Marxist can only work effectively as a member of an organized party, which has close relations with the working class and the peasantry, and which seeks to win mass backing for the policy which it pursues in the wider movement."[37] Uniting splinter groups was but the first stage in forming a "Marxist party in Nigeria [that] would aim to develop militant trade unionism . . . to create an alliance between the working class and the peasantry and to win a leading position for the working class, and the Marxist party in the broader national movement."[38]

Taking the situation as a whole, and bearing in mind all the complications of the rival Marxist groups in Nigeria, the CPGB developed four evolving guidelines throughout the 1950s. These were:

(1) Maintain friendly contact with all Marxist groups in Nigeria and all individuals interested in Marxism;

(2) Refrain from official recognition of any Marxist group, but urge all professed Marxists to unite and reach a policy and program that would speed up the formation of a Marxist Party;

(3) Ensure a more adequate supply of Marxist literature to groups and individuals, and other means of assistance for the regular publication of material in Nigeria;

(4) Regularly undertake thorough on-the-spot reviews of the fluid situation in Nigeria before making any official pronouncements.

CONCLUSION

Between the late 1950s and early 1960s, Marxists intensified their activities in Nigeria, although lacking the same momentum from earlier years. In November 1960, a group of youths made up largely of members of the

Nigerian Youth Congress formed the Communist Party of Nigeria in Kano. Official records indicate that the initial inspiration and subsequent sponsorship came from the Communist Party of Great Britain. Unfortunately, surviving records do not provide answers about, for example, why Kano was chosen over other areas, and who the group leaders were. What little information we have comes from a membership list, which while still classified as to specific names, has an aggregate total higher than that of the Communist Party of Nigeria, formed at Ibadan in 1951. Interestingly, the Kano group's constitution was based on the 1945 Constitution of the Chinese Communist Party.[39] However, whether it received financial sponsorship and political directives from the Chinese Communist Party is not yet clear, as available records remain silent on the question. The only available evidence is that financial support came through Egypt and Ghana but, contrary to contemporary official views, was most likely intended for nationalism-building purposes rather than for the promotion of Communism.

Another group identified by official intelligence reports was the "Nucleus," made up of returnees from Soviet bloc countries. This organization probably emerged in late 1959 or early 1960. Officials could not penetrate membership activities because of the group's highly secretive nature. American intelligence reported that "although small in members it presents a long-term threat to security since its leaders are indoctrinated disciplined Communists with close relations with the Soviet bloc and markedly untainted by the corruption and venality which afflicts other pseudo-Communist bodies in Nigeria."[40] In a post-independent Nigeria, communists looked to the "Nucleus" to provide the impetus for extricating the country from international capitalism. The British and their allies (including both Nigerians and Western powers initiated and effectively executed policies to prevent a pendulum swing in favor of the Nigerian Marxists.

Chapter Five
Profiling Nigerian Marxists

INTRODUCTION

Nigerian leftists were not insulated from their counterparts along the West Coast of Africa and across the Atlantic Ocean. As noble patriots, Nigerian leftists propagated their views through newspapers, intellectual debates, and political activism in youth organizations, the labor movement, and nationalist parties. It seems the ghosts of I.T.A. Wallace and Frank Macaulay remained with the Nigerian leftists throughout the 1950s and afterwards. Throughout the 1930s these men corresponded with George Padmore and *The Negro Worker* where they published articles denouncing British colonial rule in Nigeria and exposing U.S. race relations to colonial people. Frank Macaulay's untimely death in 1931 and Wallace departure for his native country, Sierra Leone, in 1933, halted Marxist orientation among Nigerians. In fact, continued hostility toward leftist ideology and the banning of Marxist, socialist, and Black radical publications from abroad only heightened interests among Nigerian leftists. It is in the light of this that a summarization of the profiles of some of the leftists is relevant.

THE FRONT-LINERS

In Chapters Three and Four we discussed the role of Marxists such as Samuel Ikoku, Ayo Ogunseye, and various Marxist organizations set up during the 1950s. In this chapter, we focus on selected individuals to buttress the view that Marxism permeated souls and minds of some Nigerians despite official opposition. The careers of Nduka Eze, Gogo Chu Nzeribe, Samuel Akpata, H.O. Davies, and Funmilayo Kuti to mention a few, in labor unionism and the nationalist movement further explain attempts by Marxists to infiltrate into sectors of the Nigerian colonial state. While there were other leftists during the same period, these men are unique in view of their credentials. Concerning Eze for instance, records from the Communist Party of Great Britain (CPGB) indicates that he was "the most outstanding" personality in "the history of the Nigerian working class movement" during the colonial era.[1]

The year 1950 remained memorable in the life of Nduka Eze. First, he established contact with the CPGB leaders such as Harry Pollitt, Margot, Barbara Ruheman, and Idris Cox, perhaps through Okafor and Onowochei who had joined the CPGB around 1946 in England. Second, he was instrumental in the publication of *Labour Champion,* the first Nigerian labor newspaper. Though short-lived, *Labour Champion* was a clear expression of Marxist influence, with a strong emphasis on the principles of international unity. Through this paper, he was in close contact with officials of the *Daily Worker,* a communist newspaper in London. In fact, he was reported to have sent one of his young reporters, Idise Dafe, to the *Daily Worker* (London) to be trained as a journalist.[2] Eze had earlier sought financial support from the British TUC in setting up the *Labour Champion* in June 1949.[3]

However, the response was negative because TUC officials were clearly informed about Eze's role in the defunct Nigerian Trades Union Congress in March 1949 and his Marxian indoctrination.[4] In fact, the Labor Adviser in Nigeria, Roberts Curry, was not in support of Eze's appeal as he viewed it as one of the Communists tactics of persons presenting themselves as pro-Western leaders in the colonies only to propagate Communist ideology through the paper. In his words: "Eze's methods are typically Communist, his speeches and press reports are very obviously inspired from outside sources."[5]

Eze was, at one time, President-General of the Zikist Movement, the Secretary of the United African Company Workers' Union and the Nigerian National Federation of Labour, a breakaway organisation from the (Nigeria) Trade Union Congress, and the Secretary of the National Scholarships Board formed in May 1950. Nduka was born in 1925 at Asaba where he attended Christian Mission schools until 1944. He soon moved to Lagos Colony and worked as a manager-in-training for United African Company (UAC). He briefly worked as an assistant editor of the *Nigerian Advocate* in 1946. In late 1946, he soon became the secretary-general of the UAC African Workers' Union overseeing employees' interest in Nigeria and the Mandated Territory of Cameroon. He took an active part in trade union activities and nationalist politics thenceforth distinguishing himself as a leader.[6]

There are conflicting reports about the circumstances that led to his exit from the UAC staff list. To the CPGB, Eze left the UAC voluntarily in

1947 after many "attempts by the management to buy[7] him off and intimidate him failed."[8] To British officials, however, many activists had indeed being sacked but for a variety of reasons including, as in Eze's case, "insubordination."[9]

As President of the Lagos branch, executive member and later President of the Zikist Movement, Eze constantly inspired and educated young men in the movement in the spirit of Marxism. He taught Marxism, not in the abstract, but in relation to the needs of the Nigerian Labour movement and the political situation in Nigeria generally. He gathered around himself a group of young men who had developed a deep interest in Marxism, composed of Osita Agwuna, O.I. Dafe, J. Onwugbuzio, Mokwugo Okoye, G. Nzeribe, I. Nzimiro, A. Ikoro, Ezuma, C.K. Opara, Mallam Abdallah, M. Kolagbodi, Chikwendu Nwariaku, and others who began to apply Marxism in their practical political activities and carried it to the labor movement.[10]

It was through many of his activities that he sought and received supports from Communist bodies in Europe. One of his activities was in connection with the selection of Nigerian students for study in East Germany and Czechoslovakia.[11] In order to succeed in this he formed the National Scholarships Board in 1950. Needless to say Eze and his group were in close contact with the Free German Youth in East Germany. The *Free German Youth* (FGY) sent a message of solidarity to Eze on the Enugu incident.[12] Moreover, the *FGY* had since 1950 made specific offers indicating that they were prepared to admit selected Nigerian students into East Germany to study at universities or secondary schools. The *FGY* also stressed that all expenses, once the students were across the German border, would be paid by them.[13]

Immediately there followed local advertisements sponsored by the newly formed National Scholarships Board under the presidency of Folarin Coker[14] and the secretary ship of Nduka Eze. An unspecified number of scholarships were allotted for university training. For secondary education, ten places were made available for applicants not exceeding fourteen years of age. Moreover, all board, tuition and lodging were free and the Scholarships Board was apparently prepared to provide passage money. Importantly, such students were to be recommended by 'democratic organisations' after the payment of a small affiliation fee.[15]

By October 1950 the Board was able to send two students, who were accompanied by one N.E. Kolagbodi, an ex-Zikist, to Berlin and Prague. And by early November 1950, about six and nine students respectively had applied for placement at secondary schools and universities in Berlin and Prague through the Board.[16] In order to expedite processing of the students' passage, Edward Onowochei, a Nigerian member of the Communist Party of Great Britain, was appointed London liaison officer for Eze's National Scholarships Board. He was in charge of student welfare and their onward passage to either Berlin or Prague.[17] In 1951, the American Consul General in Nigeria, A.W. Childs concluded that, "Onowochei was directing the entire scheme and appeared to act as liaison officer with both the Free German Youth and the Communist Party of Great Britain."[18]

In March 1951, another batch of seven students arrived in Berlin. The eighth was held up for some time by legal complications in London, but she later arrived in Berlin in April.[19] It was reported that apart from Onowochei, the CPGB and WFTU, the Czech and Soviet Embassies assisted Nigerians, as well as other colonial students' journeys to Berlin and Prague.[20]

By April 1951, a report from Germany indicated that students were provided by the Soviets with clothing, food and recreation. And, more importantly, "political science" became a mandatory course that must be taken by all students, particularly those from colonies. During the same month, fifteen students were selected for the Agricultural and Forestry Workers Scholarship in Eastern Germany.[21] By May 1951, another batch of eight students was sent to Berlin under the Scholarships Board scheme.

Despite strict observation of non-issuance of international passports to Nigerians intending to go behind the Iron Curtain, Eze's machinations seemed to succeed. A.W. Childs noted that, "in at least one and probably more cases passports have been obtained by means of forged application and blank passport forms."[22] This led to criticism of the local passport authority in Lagos for "laxness in allowing blank passports to be stolen and not controlling immigration more efficiently to prevent students from reaching Czechoslovakia, Eastern Germany and Russia."[23]

These events soon led men of the Nigerian police and the Special Branch to raid the headquarters of the NSB in July 1951. Eze and Onwurike (a beneficiary of the NSB Award) were arrested and charged with being in possession of forged passports and blank forms. Further investigations resulted in the arrest of an immigration police corporal, Ajayi Busari, in November 1951. Onwurike and Eze were fined £10 and £50 respectively for possessing a false passport. On the other hand, Busari was sentenced to three years imprisonment for theft and sale of passports and passport application forms and making false entries in the passport register.[24]

Nduka Eze was involved in labor unionism, which was his primary constituency for the greater part of his career. As he did for the Scholarships Board, he was able to gather funds for the labor movement to foster their anti-British activities. His first move in labor movement was to dislodge pro-Western leaders such as Adio-Moses from the Nigerian TUC in late 1949. His formation of the Nigerian National Federation of Labour in late 1949 was the seal of his dominance of the labor movement in Nigeria during the period. By 1950 he had affiliated the body with the World Federation of Trade Unions in Paris, and established a fraternity with the Communist Party of Great Britain.

It was through his links with the WFTU and the CPGB that he was able to get sponsorships from these bodies and other satellite groups. In early 1951, the sum of £2,300 was transferred from the Communist Third International in Prague to Ezuma's account at the Barclays Bank DC and O in Lagos. There is need for a historical background to the WFTU grant. When the *Labour Champion* could not meet its financial obligations in late 1950, it naturally died. Attempts to resuscitate it led to Eze, Ikoro, Ezuma and Nzimiro's appeal to WFTU early in 1951.

Ezuma was sent to Paris to solicit for WFTU assistance under the guise that the *Labour Champion* belonged to the Nigerian Labour Congress. Naturally, it was easy for the sympathy of the WFTU to be enlisted for the only newspaper owned by the workers of Nigeria. And more importantly they were aware about Eze's credentials as a frontline Marxist. Two errors were committed: the first was belief that the *Labour Champion* was owned by the NLC, and second, the deposit of the grant into a private account—Ezuma's.[25] It is however unfortunate that the *Labour Champion* was never resuscitated despite the receipt of the money.

The U.S. consular noted that the sum of £200 was given to the Nigerian Labour Congress on the agreement that certain Communist sympathizers were nominated to the executive of the Congress.[26] Later in the year, WFTU deposited another £2,000 into the account of the union.[27] It was thus, easy for the *Daily Times* and the *West African Pilot,* to "prove that the Communist World, far from trying to help Nigerian workers was aiming at financing disruptive activities in Nigeria."[28]

The aftermath was a crisis in the labor union and a split in *All-Nigeria Trade Union Federation* (ANTUF), which led to the emergence of new groups.[29] While those who objected to the communist fund later formed the National Council of Trade Unions, Nigeria, the Left Wing emerged under the name of Trade Union Congress, Nigeria (TUCN). The National Council of Trade Unions, Nigeria, under Borha, Adio-Moses and Adebola, were in support of an affiliation with the *International Confederation of Trade Unions* (ICFTU), while the Trade Union Congress, Nigeria, (TUCN) under Eze, Nzeribe, Imoudu and Wahab Goodluck, preferred to join the *World Federation of Trade Unions* (WFTU).[30] The split in the labor movement during the period could be interpreted as a struggle between communism and capitalism.[31]

The split did not, however, solve the problem among the Left Wing as several hundreds of workers who lost their jobs in December 1950 when a communist-organized general strike failed demanded strike and unemployment pay.[32] A member union of the Congress, the *Nigeria Brewery Workers' Union,* demanded that a General Council meeting of the Congress be called forthwith to discuss the allocation of the communist funds.[33] There was also dissension in the union as to the control and expenditure of union funds. When members of the *Trade Union Congress* began to make allegations of corruption against Eze, the colonial administration effectively used this to clamp down on him by charging him with corruption and other offences, such as passport forging.[34]

It must be stated that Eze's activities in Nigeria attracted the attention of the CPGB leaders in London. Some of them believed that he had shown some leadership quality and could lead a Marxist party if given further support. Not all CPGB leaders were in favor of Eze however. There were some who were worried about Nigeria trade union members' allegations of corruption against Eze and his vulnerability to government in this regard.

Gogo Chu Nzeribe was born in 1930 at Oguta. He was educated at the prestigious King's College, Lagos. Like Eze, he had served as councilor on the Lagos Town Council in 1950-51. Nzeribe was the founding secretary of the *All-Nigeria Trade Union Federation.*[35] He was also the Secretary General of the Union of Posts and Telecommunications Workers of Nigeria from 1952 to 1954. To British officials, Nzeribe was a rebel, while to his opponents he was a communist. To the Americans, he was "a courageous champion of the rights of the workers and certainly a radical and probably a communist sympathizer."[36]

He soon proved officials right, when, on the morning of March 19, 1958, an estimated 3,000 employees of the Posts and Telegraphs Department ceased work in response to a call to strike by Gogo Chu Nzeribe.[37] Although Nzeribe described it as a "48-hour protest demonstration" against management inefficiency and ineptitude, the government and the press described it as a communist tactic to attack the government.[38]

By this period, anti-Marxist policies had become an instrument used by many folks (both officials and non-officials) to silence opposition. The management of Posts and Telegraph were no exception to the "Nigerian-McCarthyism." They concluded that the strike was a Marxist-inspired disrespect for a peaceful labor negotiation and resolution of the situation. While not denying Nzeribe's socialist inclination, management's conclusion of the strike as being sponsored by Communists is however suspect and inaccurate. It nonetheless highlights the fear of the Nigerian Federal Labour Minister, Okotie-Eboh, in July 1957 concerning the potentials of Gogo Chu Nzeribe.[39]

The strike was significant in several respects. Firstly, it was the most efficiently organized and most widely based strike to have occurred in the country in several years. Secondly, the secrecy with which the strike was arranged, taking the public and the government by complete surprise, was little short of astounding. Thirdly, one can say that the complete ruthlessness and disregard for public welfare, which characterized the strike suggests, and was condemned by the press, as communist tactics.[40] Nigerian administrators and politicians who had assumed partial governance during the mid-1950s did not take kindly to leftist ideology in labor unions. To the Permanent Secretary of the Ministry of Labour and Welfare, Francis Nwokedi, "the disruptive tactics employed by Nzeribe were typically communist," and to the Prime Minister, Tafawa Balewa, "the government probably underestimated him."[41]

Another closely monitored and highly educated communist during the period was Samuel Bankole Akpata. Born in Lagos in 1920, Akpata was educated at Umuahia Government College, and Yaba Higher College, where he spent two years. From Yaba, he went to the United Kingdom in 1941 to study at London University. It was there that he associated with *W.A.S.U; Communist Party of Great Britain; World Federation of Democratic Youth, International Union of Students,* and the *Free German Youth.*

By late 1945 he had been elected into the executive of the WFDY. Also in late 1945, Akpata was involved in the formation of the West African National Secretariat. The antecedent was a secret meeting held with Nkrumah, Botsio, Nikoi, Wallace and Awooner-Renner in London.

At the meeting, the party agreed to "form a radical progressive organisation for seizing power in Africa as quickly as possible." Their ultimate aim was "national unity, independence and a union of African Socialist Republic."[42] He was an assistant secretary, and later secretary, of the WANS in early 1947. He also supported the Gold Coast Students Union rally at Trafalgar Square on March 8, 1948, where he denounced the colonial Government's handling of the February 1948 riot in Accra.[43]

The *Communist Party of the Soviet Union* later offered him a scholarship to read for his Masters and Ph.D. at the Charles University, Prague, in 1949. Between 1949 and 1953 he attended various communist conferences, among them the *World Federation of Democratic Youth* conference in Budapest in 1949, where he claimed to represent *Youth Congress of Nigeria,* and the communist organized Berlin Conference of 1951. He returned to Nigeria in July 1953 and was appointed Secretary General of the *Railway*

Workers Union on a salary of £240 per annum.[44] At the height of his career, he became the Librarian of the University College, Ibadan.[45]

Anglo-American intelligence reports also focused on a prominent Queen's lawyer, H.O. Davies. A Lagosian, Davies studied law in London and was called to the bar before returning to Nigeria. His activities as a member of the West African Students Union during the 1920s is well documented and need not be repeated here.[46] Davies, more than anyone else, was the defender of the radicals and professed Marxists in Nigeria during the period under review. Apart from his legal work, he formed an embryonic political party called the *People's Congress Party*. He also established a newspaper called *The Nigerian People's Voice*.[47] The *PCP* seems to have had two major planks in its platform: a denunciation of Nigerian tribalism and regionalism, and support of the workers with a "self characterization of being the friend of the workers."[48]

Robert Ross, the American vice consul, summarized the place of Davies during the period under review thus: " . . . a man to watch on the local political scene as a potentially strong leader of the Leftist elements of the politically conscious minority in Nigeria. He might well become a likely candidate to fill the position of chief communist contact because of his very high intellect and political maturity."[49] Ironically, Ross was proved wrong by later events as Davies pitched camp with Azikiwe in the *NCNC*, a party considered, like the *Action Group* and the *Northern People's Congress,* as favoring constitutional and gradual decolonization, rather than the revolutionary liberation of Nigeria.[50] He, like Azikiwe, opted for Fabian socialism and pragmatic ideas that preached non-violence. This was one of the ways through which Azikiwe contained the Leftists in the NCNC.[51]

We should note that Ross was not the only one that was proved wrong. Leaders of the Communist Party of Great Britain (who had hoped for his leadership of a Marxist group that would metamorphose into a Nigeria Communist party) were also disappointed about his liberal attitude towards British rule in Nigeria after 1945. Davies had been close with some British members of the CPGB during the World War II and immediately after.

He was reported to have visited the CPGB office while in London as a student. The case of Davies is that of someone in search of knowledge. He was interested in knowing about Marxism and communism and whether it could be adapted to the situation in the colony. A CPGB document in late 1951 titled; "Draft Discussion on the Nature and Personnel of the Leadership of the Nigerian Trade Union and National Movement," highlights the disappointment of the organization about Davies' switch to the right.[52]

Their hope in him as a leader of a Marxist group was dashed as he joined the NCNC. Leaders of the CPGB concluded that Davies "character as a Yoruba separatist and splitter of the national movement is now so well known that it requires no further comment."[53]

Furthermore, anxiety about communism during the 1950s can be seen in the way Funmilayo Ransome-Kuti was treated by the government. The wife of Reverend Ransome-Kuti, Funmilayo was, perhaps, the most vocal and radically educated woman in Nigeria during the devolution period. She and her husband had been exposed internationally through close contacts with Ladipo Solanke (founder of WASU), Reginald Sorenson, Arthur and Violet Creech Jones, Freda Grimble, and the Labour Party leadership before 1947.[54] It has to be noted that none of these people was remotely connected with communism. They nonetheless inspired her in her attitude and perception of British rule in Nigeria.

She was included as a member of the *NCNC* delegation to London in 1947 to present the views of the party on the Richards Constitution to the Secretary of State for the Colonies. It was during this period that she joined the *Women's International Democratic Federation (WIDF)*, a USSR inspired organization founded in Paris in 1945. Its aims were to "unite women regardless of race, nationality, religion and political opinion, so that they may work together to win, implement and defend national independence and democratic freedoms, eliminate apartheid, racial discrimination and fascism; work for peace and universal disarmament."[55]

Between 1946 and 1957, Funmilayo was involved in the *WIDF* activities. She, in fact, contributed a chapter in a communist sponsored book in 1948 where she criticized British rule in Nigeria and called for the improvement of women's condition in the colonies and protectorates.[56] She attended a *WIDF* conference in Vienna on the defense of children on April 9, 1952, as well as participated during the Copenhagen Congress in June 1953 where she was elected as one of the vice-presidents of the *WIDF.* Her paper was published along with others in 1954 by WIDF entitled "*That They May Live: African Women Arise.*" It was no surprise that, the government banned *WIDF* literature in July 1954 after the visit of the organization's Secretary General to Funmilayo at Abeokuta in the same month.[57]

With her international connections, she formed an embryonic organization called the *National Women's Union* (NWU) in 1952, through which she sought to educate women about their socio-economic conditions under the British rule. It is worthy of note that, under Funmilayo, the NWU successfully organized women against a government water rate levy in Abeokuta district in 1952.

Such activities only allowed government to see her as a radical and a communist sympathizer. And in 1955, she was refused a passport to travel to Helsinki, Finland, to attend a communist sponsored World Assembly of Peace.[58]

Funmilayo was also actively involved with other radical and socialist inclined organizations during and after the colonial period. As far back as 1949, Funmilayo had contacted Marcus Garvey's United Negro Improvement Association's Women's Corp.[59] She also corresponded with women in Trinidad, Korea and Vietnam. In Africa, she visited the Gold Coast (Ghana) several times and assisted in the formation of its Women's Movement in 1960.[60]

Her quest for women development was also instrumental in her joining the British Women's International Association, a non-communist organization in 1952. Although McGregor Wood, leader of BWIA was skeptical about Funmilayo's ideological leaning, Solanke assured her that "Mrs. Funmilayo Ransome-Kuti is not a communist."[61] This assurance from the WASU leader and Funmilayo's correspondence with Wood was instrumental in the acceptance of her membership and the affiliation of the Nigerian Women Association to BWIA.

Funmilayo's case shows that some nationalists were only interested in how they could benefit from some international organizations as a means towards achieving their set goal. While it has been difficult to identify other nationalists in this category, one can argue that it was a miscalculation for any nationalist to have joined a pro-communist organization during the period. While official intelligence reports maintained that she was a communist, her biographers are of the view that Funmilayo was a pragmatist unwilling to be controlled by any of them (East or West).[62]

Although she was allowed to visit Peking in 1956 to attend a *WIDF* council meeting, her passport was not endorsed for the 1957 *WIDF* conference. It should be stressed that leading nationalists who occupied high office during the mid-1950s maintained anti-leftist measures hitherto in place. Official non-endorsement of Funmilayo's passport drew many criticisms, as it was a restriction of individual freedom of movement and expression. In response Balewa, as the Head of Government Business (later Prime Minister) remarked that "in the past when it was thought Mrs. Kuti might be an innocent victim of communist schemes, she was informed officially . . . but now it can be assumed that it is her intention to influence the various Nigerian women's organizations with which she is connected with communist ideas and policies . . . On those grounds the government would not renew her passport."[63] Despite her protests, Balewa's government did not change its decision until after independence when approval was given for the renewal of her passport.[64]

CONCLUSION

To conclude, Marxism and leftist ideology generally was seen as a threat to the sustenance of a "nurtured capitalism" in Nigeria and the survival of a worldwide capitalism. In Nigeria during the period under review, some of the labor leaders particularly the younger elements imbibed the leftist ideology. The ideology of the left assumed a potent force within the labor and trade unions largely because of the activities of people like Eze, Nzeribe, Akpata, Bassey, Imoudu, and Wahab Goodluck. With the banning of the Zikist Movement in April 1950, efforts to rejuvenate Marxist ideas within the nationalist and labor groups were met with counter-measures by the central and regional governments. Hence Marxist organizations that emerged afterwards enjoyed, at best, a suspended animation as they found it difficult to co-exist with the stiff government measures.[65] Henceforth, leftist groups' efforts to gain minimal success were met with anti-leftist policies initiated from time to time by colonial government, and later post-colonial pro-Western governments, at the central and regional levels.

Chapter Six
"Nigeria-McCarthyism": No Job for the Red?[1]

INTRODUCTION

Post-war colonial policies in British West Africa were predicated on the success of official initiatives about colonial development, race relations, devolution, and the eventual transfer of power. Success, however, involved measures aimed at destroying any form of radical nationalism. Colonial officials were concerned about growing leftist nationalism, increasing Marxist literature in the colonies, and funds from a Communist network into the colonies during the decolonization era. Both colonial and nationalist governments were bent on preventing leftists from being employed in the public service. These measures can be described as "Nigeria-McCarthyism."

METROPOLITAN INITIATIVES

In 1950, Nigeria was placed in the special category of front-line colonies because "it had become a major object of Soviet Cold War attention."[2] On May 1, 1951, Governor John Macpherson requested approval from James Griffiths, the secretary of state for the colonies, to ban communists from government employment.[3] Griffiths' response was that the Nigerian Council of Ministers should deliberate on the matter. However, it was not until May 25, 1954, that the federal Council of Ministers asked for the submission of a paper on steps that might be taken against communist infiltration into the civil service and trade union movement. It seems that this was provoked by Dr. Kwame Nkrumah's speech at the Gold Coast Legislative Assembly on February 25, 1954, in which he stated that his government would in the future refuse to employ in certain branches of the public service persons who had proved to be active communists.[4] These branches were the administrative, education, community development, labor, information services, police, army, and the Gold Coast commissioners' Offices overseas. Two years later Nkrumah was proud to say that "the infiltration by Communist agents into 'our workers' organisations has now been completely checked."[5]

The background to colonial government's ban on the employment of Communists and fellow travelers cannot be fully understood without elaborating the metropolitan initiatives. Despite the Labour government's past relationship with the Communist Party and the Labor movement generally, the British (and the colonial government) government was sincere in its anti-Communist positions. Participants at the various Labour Party annual conferences during the 1940s noted the fundamental differences between the Labour Party and the Communist Party of Great Britain. As one participant put it: " . . . our Party seeks to achieve Socialism by persuasion and the ballot boxes in contrast to the Communist party doctrine of the overthrow of capitalism by armed force if necessary . . ."[6] This partly explains the futile attempts to affiliate the Communist Party with the Labour Party during the 1946 and 1947 conferences.[7]

It should not be surprising, therefore, that the foundation of anti-leftist sanctions and measures was laid under a Labour government. Clement Attlee, the British prime minister, announced on the floor of the House of Commons on March 15, 1948, that: " . . . A civil servant suspected of membership or association with the Communist Party or a Fascist organization in such a way as to raise legitimate doubts of his reliability, shall be summarily dismissed or transferred to less sensitive sector of the National parastatals."[8]

In an answer to a question during the debate, Attlee maintained that "Experience, both in this country and elsewhere, has shown that membership of, and other forms of continuing association with, the Communist Party may involve the acceptance by the individual of a loyalty, which in certain circumstances can be inimical to the State."[9]

Although acknowledging the difficulty of reading the minds of men, the prime minister maintained that "there is no way of distinguishing such people from those who, if opportunity offered, would be prepared to endanger the security of the State in the interests of another Power."[10] Suffice it to say that this policy applied to Communists and fellow travelers, excluding Fabian-Socialists, who controlled the Labour Party. This gave the opposition (Conservatives) room for criticism, as they opined that Socialism is a transitory stage to Communism. They also criticized the government's secret trial of suspected Communists or fellow travelers maintaining that it was against democracy.[11]

Such criticism did not stop Attlee and his cabinet from executing the policy. As he graphically noted: "I say that, owing to the fact that they have a different loyalty, they cannot serve the State."[12] By mid-1948, Sir W. Smithers, representing Orpington in the House of Commons, had called on the government "to take effective steps to outlaw Communism in this country," rather than what he called, "fiddling about with the Civil Service."[13] And at the Annual Labour Party conference in 1948, a majority of the members present supported government action.[14]

Lord Vansittart again raised the matter on the floor of the House of Lords in March 1950. In his address titled "Communists in the Public Service," Lord Vansittart reiterated the government position and noted "continuous and resolute precautions are necessary for public security."[15] Lord Milverton, formerly governor of Nigeria, supported him when he noted, "There is no room for Communism in the world."[16] Some, however, were mild in their criticism of the communists. To the Earl of Iddlesleigh, "Communists are better left alone to continue their loud orations in order not to drive them underground."[17]

Despite their criticism of some aspects of the policy, the Conservative government also pursued anti-leftist policies. Keeping leftist ideology within bounds was seen as a step toward preserving democratic freedoms *a la* Westminster. In the colonies, both nationalist and labor leaders were expected to be wholeheartedly anti-leftist. Any suspicious act could reverse the course of development in the colonies as in the case of British Guiana in 1953.[18]

As Sir T. Lloyd (permanent under secretary, 1947–1956) noted: "Events in British Guiana have shown that their (Communists) tactics may take the form of building up and practicing Communism while denying that they are Communists, not only to the World at large but also to their own followers."[19] He concluded that "A small minority of determined Communists will do everything to exercise the greatest possible influence and they will use that influence solely for the purposes of disruption. This is not a remote danger, but a very near one."[20]

In West Africa, nationalist governments were encouraged to make policies aimed at curtailing Communism. Like Tafawa Balewa, K. Nkrumah also propped up some labor leaders as fronts in his anti-Communist crusade. He initiated the merger between the Gold Coast TUC and the Ghana TUC in order to place his supporters in advantaged positions in the new labor union.[21]

Nkrumah, however, did not succeed immediately in checking the activities of Communists such as C. Woode, Q. Ocran, and G. Kumah in the new Ghana TUC that emerged.[22] By early 1954, however, Nkrumah and his cabinet had succeeded in expelling known Communists such as Woode and Ocran from the CPP, as well as instituting the vetting procedure in civil service appointments. As Rathbone rightly concludes, "the adoption of these apparently draconian measures by the CPP dominated government was only partly intended to reassure the Conservative government in London."[23]

By February 18, 1954, Oliver Lyttelton, the Colonial Secretary, informed the cabinet at Whitehall that the Gold Coast government under Nkrumah had taken the following steps: (1) "Ban the entry of all Communist literature into the Gold Coast," (2) "Exclude any European with Communist sympathies from the public service and exclude any African with Communist sympathies from a certain number of Departments like the Administration, the police and the Department of Education;" (3) "Confiscate the passports of the few Gold Coast Communists who wish to travel behind the Iron Curtain."[24]

In Nigeria, it was recognized that the most effective prophylactic against leftist ideology was the education of the community as to its aims and objectives. Leftist ideology was not only opposed to the pace of decolonization, but its ultimate goal of independence within the Commonwealth. In view of the leftists' in-roads into labor unions, the Council of Ministers noted that the greatest danger lay within organized labor.[25]

On October 18, 1954, both Federal and Regional Governments took a step further in their anti-leftist measures when they finally resolved to place a ban on the employment of communists and their sympathizers in the public service. On October 19, 1954, J.O. Field, principal assistant secretary of the federation, and J.S. Dudding, senior assistant secretary for security and defense, addressed a press conference on government policy on leftist ideology.[26] A press statement was released, captioned "Council of Ministers Report"; it was published as "Government Notice No.1769: Statement of policy on the employment of communists in the public services." It read thus:

> After careful examination of the situation in Nigeria and in other countries, particularly those in the British Commonwealth . . . the Council of Ministers has reached the conclusion that steps are necessary to prevent the infiltration of active communists into posts in the service of the country in which divided loyalty might be dangerous to the interests of Nigeria. The first loyalty of a communist lies not to Nigeria, but to a foreign communist organization, the objective of which is the political, economic and social subjugation of Nigeria. The Governments of Nigeria are therefore of the opinion that persons who are indoctrinated with

communism should not be permitted to occupy posts in the service of Government in which it is possible for them to further the ends of the organization to which they owe allegiance. It has therefore proved to the satisfaction of Government that active communists will in the future not be employed in the following branches of the Nigerian Public Services: Administration, Education, Labour, Police, Posts and Telegraphs, Railway, Civil Aviation, or in certain key posts in other branches of the Public Services.[27]

Both active Communists and their sympathizers in Nigeria were taken into consideration. Another point in the policy statement was the remark that employers of labor should also take steps to prevent communist penetration of the commercial sector.[28] During this period, about ten communists were identified as being in the public service, while not less than two hundred were said to be out of the public service.[29] Some newspapers' comments were favorable to the government's decision. An editorial in the *Daily Service* of October 16, 1954, captured the mood of the press. It noted, "Based on the past performances of Communists in non-communist countries, we fully endorse the principle outlined in the statement, but we will add that other positive approaches must be made to combat the growth of communism. You may not give active communist job (sic), but that will not stop communism from growing. What will stop it is to carry out social programs that will build an educated public in a prosperous Country and will also eradicate social injustice. Communism thrives on ignorance and poverty."[30]

To the *West African Pilot*, owned by Dr. N. Azikiwe, the best recipe against leftist ideology was not repression or persecution but rather the "application of a more powerful ideology which is based on moral goodness on the part of those who govern and those who are governed, thus leading ultimately to real existence of freedom of thought, speech or association."[31]

The success of the government's measures cannot be over-emphasized. As the American consul Herbert T. Krueger noted in January 1956, "The drastic decrease in the shipment of such propaganda, as compared to the 1953-early 1954 period, attests to the effectiveness of the ban on communist publications" and the employment of communists in the civil service.[32]

Marxist leaders, both in Nigeria and Great Britain, felt the effect of this policy. The situation was not helped by deteriorating race relations between CPGB leaders and Nigerian members who had complained about "arrogance" among the leaders. The Nigerian government's ban on the employment of communists, announced in October 1954, further reduced the morale of some Nigerian members of the CPGB who had earlier thought about resigning from the body. As Adi rightly notes: "In 1954, the decline in membership was no doubt accelerated by an announcement by the Federal and Regional governments in Nigeria, that no known Communist would be employed in essential public service or in the civil service."[33]

Meanwhile, at its meeting of December 29, 1954, the federal Council of Ministers took further action to ban communists from the public service by applying much the same screening methods that had been used at the University College, Ibadan, since 1951, for the appointment of Nigerians and expatriates in the public sector.[34] The measure included screening through the special force and police CID names of candidates for civil service jobs. In a conversation with the American consul-general McLauglin, Azikiwe remarked that the measure had succeeded throughout the country and particularly in his area of control (Eastern Region).[35]

In May 1955, the Eastern Region Ministry of Education circulated a notice to all private schools receiving government support to the effect that State funds would be withdrawn from those schools which continued to employ Communist teachers after December 31, 1955.[36] Awolowo also confirmed that the measure had succeeded in the Western Region and Lagos where most of the communists and their sympathizers lived and worked. Unlike Azikiwe, he added that the governments had been over zealous about the whole matter.[37]

COMMERCIAL FIRMS AND ORGANIZED LABOR

A leading labor leader once remarked that, "The initial and most embarrassing problem is that the workers are wont (sic) to look up to Communist and Communist influenced International Labour Organisations for material and financial aid." He stated further that, "The psychological frailty and weakness of the average Nigerian worker, which—virtually—are engendered by want, insecurity and manumission, constitute the most fertile soil on which the baneful doctrine Communism thrives than ever."[38]

The percentage of the Nigerian working class was put at 3 percent of the total population in 1954. An official figure indicates that there was 152,000 trade union members organized in 116 trade unions. Seven of the unions had more than 5,000 members. These were the Nigerian Union of Teachers (26,000); Amalgamated Union of the United Africa Company Workers Union (19,000); Public Utility Technical and General Workers Union of Nigeria and the Cameroons (12,000); Nigeria African Mineworkers Union (11,000); Railway Workers Union (11,000); and the Nigerian Civil Service Union (6,000).[39]

As the figures show, a majority of Nigerian workers were employed by the colonial government, which thus gave them a key position to exercise pressure on British rule. To Nigerian Marxists, a trade union member should not stand aloof in the struggle against imperialism as practiced by the British. They seem to have imbibed the doctrine laid down by the CPGB leaders. As the CPGB leaders noted in one of their political ideological classes, "Non-political trade unionism is a betrayal of the interests of the workers and of the national struggle."[40] They, however, realized government's determined effort to keep "trade unions subservient to the employers and the Government, and to keep them isolated from the national struggle."[41]

Having noted that the sector of the society most vulnerable to leftist ideology was the labor and trade union, the government took three major steps in an effort to combat the menace. These were the training of labor and industrial officers; the encouragement of the International Confederation of Trade Unions (ICFTU) instead of the World Federation of Trade Unions (WFTU); and the encouragement of a pro-Western labor congress through the support of activists like Cole, Adebola, Borha, Adio-Moses, Porbeni, and Labinjoh.

The British colonial administration's effort at guiding and building trade unions and industrial relations in the colonies, however, predates East-West ideological differences. Lord Passfied (Sidney Webb), the secretary of state for the colonies, in a dispatch to colonial governors in 1930 warned them " . . . to deal with trade unions with a spirit of tolerance and understanding." Regarding trade union development, he noted that " . . . there is a danger that, without sympathetic supervision and guidance, organization of laborers without experience . . . may fall under the domination of disaffected persons, by whom their activities may be diverted to improper and mischievous ends."[42] This was the genesis of government intervention in molding labor unionism in the colonies.

The 1930s saw the appointment of a labor adviser to the secretary of state, the creation of labor inspectorates (later departments), and the appointments of trade union officers "to guide and train leaders in the art and practice of trade unionism" in the colonies.[43] These were some of the objectives of the Trade Union Ordinance of 1938. During the war, efforts of the inspector of labor in Nigeria, C.H. Crossdale, were aimed at nurturing the various unions for war needs and the maintenance of sound industrial relations between the government and European employers.[44] In fact, labor and welfare officers were often sent to sensitive government parastatals to act as the bridge between the government and its employees.[45]

The Nigeria colonial government provided the lead by awarding scholarships to Nigerians to train at the University of London or under the British TUC. Between the late 1940s and 1952, eleven scholarships were awarded to Nigerians in this respect.[46] The United States Foreign Leaders Grant was also made available in the training of some Nigerians in U.S. colleges and universities in labor and industrial relations. One of the first beneficiaries was Matthew Ayodele Tokunboh. Having benefited from the government scholarship during World War II to study at the London School of Economics, he was selected for the U.S. Leaders Grant to study labor and industrial relations at Cornell University in Ithaca, New York. He rose to the post of a labor officer by the late 1940s. Other beneficiaries included Adio-Moses, Beyioku, Cole, Olugbake, and Porbeni.[47]

Between 1950 and 1960, the Department of Extra-Mural Studies of the University College, Ibadan, was charged with providing local courses/programs for future labor officers and unionists. This task was given to Ayodele Tokunboh, its first director (1950–1957). Although the literature used was provided by the U.S. Department of Labor, the British TUC, the British Council, the USIS, and the Colonial Office, the participants at the departmental conference in 1953 advised that, "courses should not appear to have been sponsored, arranged, or unduly influenced by Government."[48] Also, session lecturers were invited to give lectures on trade unionism and industrial relations. These included Nancy Sears (LSE), W. Hood (British TUC), E. Hannah (US Trade Union official), G. McRay (Trade Union College, Kampala), and G. Paxton (British TUC).[49]

In 1957 the Department of Labor also introduced "Training Within Industry" (TWI) courses in job instructions and job relations involving industrial relations, apprenticeship, training and factory organization. And by 1959, the department had been assisted by H. Tulaz, of the British TUC, in establishing a trade union school in Lagos where courses were conducted in trade union and industrial relations.[50] While it is difficult to ascertain government success in this direction, one can say that it left no stone unturned in its desire to build pro-Western trade unions.

Another agent of government in its drive towards creating pro-Western trade unionists was the International Confederation of Trade Unions (ICFTU). As early as March 1949, Roberts Curry, the labor adviser in Nigeria, had written to Vincent Tewson, the British TUC secretary, concerning the activities of the WFTU in Nigeria and the need for TUC/ICFTU initiatives. Curry noted that: "The W.F.T.U. will now be concentrating its energies on the backward countries and I have grave suspicions that Nigeria is one of the fertile grounds for their activities." He concluded that "The Government . . . is very concerned about the matter and I am advising Government on the methods to combat this menace of Communism from spreading its ugly head amongst these simple people."[51]

Early in January 1950, J. Oldenboek, the general secretary of the ICFTU, wrote to the secretary of state, Creech Jones, to support the visit of a panel of the ICFTU to British territories in Central and West Africa later in the year.[52] The primary motive was to assist in the development of free and democratic trade unions. At its executive board meeting of November 1950, it was resolved that the goal of the ICFTU was to wrest the initiative from the communists and communist-led trade unions, a goal to which it was prepared to devote substantial resources.[53] The British Trade Union Congress (TUC) and labor officers in Nigeria supported this move.[54] On November 20, 1950, Sir Vincent Tewson of the TUC wrote to the secretary of state for the colonies that the TUC would be holding a meeting with the ICFTU in Douala toward the end of January 1951 in order to prevent a similar plan by WFTU.[55]

In view of its concern about communism in Nigeria, the Gold Coast, Sierra Leone, and the Gambia, the British TUC sent a six-person delegation to these countries, prior to the Douala conference, to study the level of communist penetration with the aim of detaching them from WFTU and bringing them into the orbit of the ICFTU.[56] In fact, out of £250,000 raised to combat communism, the British TUC was said to have contributed a sum of £100,000.[57] The secretary of state for the colonies was delighted about the British TUC/ICFTU initiative since it was difficult for government to become directly involved in labor matters. Accordingly, administering officers, particularly in Nigeria where Eze's Labour Congress had affiliated with the WFTU, were directed to give every support to the delegation.[58]

The response from Nigeria was very swift. Accommodation and transport were arranged at the expense of the Nigerian government. In order not to create fear in labor circles and to disguise its anti-WFTU motive from the labor movement, the government insisted that only the ICFTU and not the government would carry out publicity for the ICFTU visit.[59] The ICFTU/TUC trip from London was, however, funded by the colonial office.[60] The endeavor was seen as an important stabilizing influence on trade union movement that would provide valuable combat against leftist ideology infiltration into the movement.[61]

On February 15, 1951, the ICFTU delegation arrived in Nigeria to propagate the aims of free democracy. These included, verbatim: (1) To inform trade union groups of the purposes and aims of the ICFTU; (2) To obtain the maximum interests and support for the West African Trade Union Conference to be held at Douala between 26th and 28th February 1951; (3) To endeavor to win over groups at present supporting the communist-controlled WFTU;

and, (4) To inform the ICFTU on labor conditions and the stage of trade union development in West Africa.[62]

Although they had some difficulties, it seems, however, that they succeeded in most respects in Nigeria and indeed other British West African colonies.[63] The task of the ICFTU/TUC in combating leftist group in organized labor was to bolster the moderate and responsible elements in colonial labor unions. It was also to encourage the production of more leaders opposed to WFTU interference. The first step in this direction was the setting up of an Information and Advice Center in Accra, which became a regional office of the body.[64] A second significant effort of the ICFTU during this period was its support for the Adio-Moses, Borha, Adebola, and Esua groups in their efforts to establish a pro-Western trade union. Despite Nduka Eze's attempt at bargaining for financial assistance as a prelude to withdrawing his section of the union's affiliation with the WFTU, the ICFTU delegation under Fred Dalley of the British TUC was only willing to assist Adio-Moses' group. It is not surprising that Adio-Moses, E. Cowan, and A. Cole were selected to represent Nigeria at the Douala meeting.[65] Adio-Moses later offered a motion at the Douala meeting on March 7, 1951 that the ICFTU should establish regional machinery for the coordination of trade union training in West and Central Africa, including the establishment of trade union colleges and the promotion of lectures. These proposals were adopted and machinery was set in motion to counter the communist influence in labor movements.[66]

By the end of 1951, Adio-Moses—with the assistance of Cowan, Borha, and Cole—had been able to gain some ground within the Nigerian labor movement.[67] An action committee was set up under Adio-Moses through which the conference recommendations were carried out. The "Action Committee" or "The Council of Action" as it was variously referred to in the TUC record, aimed at (1) Formation of a democratic national center; and, (2) Building up of branches similar to British TUC/ICFTU unions.[68] One step toward achieving these goals was the setting up of trade union educational committees and mini-libraries at trade union secretariats in major parts of the country, with books supplied by the TUC.[69]

It should be noted that Adio-Moses had been one of the beneficiaries of TUC scholarships as far back as 1947. Based on the advice of the TUC Colonial Advisory Committee, the general council offered him a scholarship to study trade unionism and industrial relations at Ruskin College, Oxford. Adio had earlier benefited from the TUC Educational Trust Fund, which enabled him to spend some time attending meetings, lectures and conferences in England.[70] In addition, there were beneficiaries from other parts of the British colonies during the period.

Activities of the ICFTU were felt in all parts of colonial Africa (and indeed in independent African states) during the period. Apart from its regional office in Accra, which published *Africa Labour* (known later as *Labour Africa Survey*), conferences and lectures were organized from time to time to ensure a democratic trade unionism on the continent. One such conference was the All-African Conference on trade unionism held at Accra between January 14 and 18, 1956. According to the organizers, it was part of initiatives toward combating the leftist ideology or any WFTU activities in Africa.[71] The opening of the Labour College at Kampala, Uganda, in November 1958 complemented this.[72]

In addition to the offer of scholarships to colonial trade unionists, the TUC general council assisted colonial trade union movements in the provision of educational facilities for their members in the form of Ruskin College correspondence courses. These were made available to trade unionists in the West Indies, West Africa, Burma and Malaya, with the TUC meeting the cost.[73] The TUC also supported extra-mural courses at the London School of Economics and Political Science, as it did for the Ruskin College, Glasgow, Southampton, and Manchester Universities.[74] The essence was to aid government efforts in building sound industrial relations and labor unions as a step toward combating leftist menace.

Between 1946 and 1952, seventeen Nigerians benefited from TUC training facilities for overseas trade unionists. Of the fifty-two places in the general training courses since its inception in 1946/47, twelve were allotted to Nigeria, nine to Germany, six to India, four to the West Indies, three to Norway and Trinidad, two to Burma and Sierra Leone, and one each to the Gold Coast, Kenya, British Guiana, Malaya, Australia, Belgium, Sweden, Greece, Southern Rhodesia, Kenya, and Holland.[75]

The private sector was not left out in the overall attempts to curtail leftist ideology in the colonies generally. European firms were generally apprehensive of communist infiltration of their workers' unions. In England, they formed a pressure group called the Overseas Employers Federation. Through this organization they were able to press for more official sanctions against any form of leftist ideology. These included Bank of British West Africa Limited, Barclays Bank (D.C.O), British and French Bank, John Holt, Rowntree-Fry-Cadbury, UAC, Elder Dempster, and Peterson Zochonis.[76] They cooperated with the labor department and the British TUC on ways to build sound industrial and labor relations.

In response to Lyttelton's request of December 9, 1953, for cooperation between the CO and the TUC, the TUC General Council met with government officials on January 28, 1954, to work out modules of operation. It was agreed that private firms had a part to play in the development of good industrial relations. To that end, it was suggested that the colonial office should meet the representatives of the Overseas Employers Federation. This was to be followed by a meeting between the three bodies.[77]

In a meeting in 1954 between the OEF, the CO, and the British TUC, it was agreed that steps against leftist ideology in colonial labor unions should remain secret.[78] In a response to A. Mellor, the director of the United Africa Company, the secretary of state for the colonies stressed however that "while it was communism which made the job so urgent . . . communism itself could only be met by developing sound industrial relations."[79]

Leading commercial firms in Nigeria, such as the Lever Brothers, the Leventis Group, John Holt Ltd, the United Africa Company, Van Der Bergh, and Elder Dempster, supported government anti-Communist measures through their disposition to notable Marxist labor leaders. For instance, the management of Lever Brothers and Van Der Bergh did not recognize Wahab Goodluck as the representative of their workers' union during a trade dispute in 1957 partly because he was tagged a communist.[80]

During the talks with the commissioner of labor, management stated categorically "all we had done was to prevent a communist from causing industrial chaos by being allowed unrestricted access to our premises."[81] The management of Lever Brothers and Van Der Bergh sought the support of the government in upholding their decision to restrict Goodluck and his cohorts from their premises, since, in their view, "government was serious in its declared attitude towards communism."[82]

The director of Elder Dempster Lines Limited, Bruce Glasier, was also concerned about the activities of Wari Orumbie (a.k.a. Sidi Omar Khayam), who was believed to have the backing of a Trotskyite group in Liverpool, to disrupt cordial labor relations between staff and management of Elder Dempster in Lagos.[83] The background to this was the seamen's strike on board the *M.V. Apapa* at Liverpool in 1957 and the subsequent dismissal of the workers by the management of Elder Dempster.[84]

By November 1958, Orumbie had successfully staged a walkout in Lagos, which disrupted the activities of the company. Elder Dempster's tactics were to sponsor other workers to disrupt the activities of Orumbie. In this the company was successful.[85] To the government, however, the most plausible counter to leftist group and organizations was the building of sound industrial relations between management and the workers.

Further government attempts at eliminating leftists' gain, if any, can be seen in their fostering of the National Council of Trade Unions, Nigeria (NCTUN) under Cole in 1957.[86] The background was N. Watson's memorandum of 1953 where he argued "it is no use trying to break communist leaders if there is nobody to step into their places."[87] He maintained that "quite apart . . . from any repressive or deterrent action in the administrative, legal or propaganda fields that H.M.G. or Colonial Governments may be able to take, the fact will always remain that resistance to communist infiltration must come from within the trade union movement itself."[88] As the secretary of state for the colonies summed it up "it is by influence and persuasion that the work would have to be done."[89]

Like Nkrumah in the Gold Coast (Ghana), Balewa's government secretly sponsored activists like Labinjoh, Adebola, and Borha to join the leftists dominated All-Nigerian Trade Union Federation (ANTUF).[90] The return of these men to the ANTUF led to the resignation of Gogo Chu Nzeribe and his cohorts from the body and the temporary declaration of ANTUF support for ICFTU.[91] But for Adebola this was not enough, the goal of the ICFTU at the Douala meeting was not to create another faction in the ANTUF but "to clean out the minority communist group and preserve ANTUF."[92]

The argument was that irrespective of the resignation of Nzeribe and his cohorts, Wahab Goodluck and Sunday Bassey still held official positions that could only be wrested from them only through an election. The solution, according to Adebola, was that "ANTUF must be completely dissolved; a new center probably reverting to the old name of Nigerian Trade Union Congress, would be formed with the NCTUN as the nucleus; and membership would be considered individually and no union harboring known pro-Communist elements in its executive would be eligible for affiliation."[93]

These machinations soon paid dividends. On March 7, 1959, approximately one hundred and fifty labor leaders representing seventy unions met at Enugu, Eastern Region, to organize a new trade union organization. With the exception of M. Imoudu, who was elected president-general of the new Trade Union Congress of Nigeria (TUC), all of the officers of the new organization had been previously closely associated with NCTUN (an anti-leftist group).[94] L. Borha, who defeated S. Bassey, secretary-general of ANTUF, by eighty-five votes to fifty-two, captured the important position of secretary-general.[95] The deputy president-General elect was S.I. Eze, president of the Nigerian Transport Staff Union affiliate of NCTUN. O. Zudonu was elected first vice-president, and O. Egwunwoke as treasurer. The former was president, and the latter, secretary of the Marine Floating Staff Union, which was affiliated with NCTUN. It should be noted that both men had earlier visited the United States and Caux (Switzerland) as strong supporters of the Moral Re-armament Movement.[96]

To achieve this sweep of important offices in the TUC, supporters of NCTUN are said to have caucused both before and during the merger and adopted a common policy.[97] As Theo Adams, the American consul, noted, "an internal split among ANTUF representatives to the conference combined with an apathy toward ANTUF on the part of the regional leaders defeated their aspirants."[98] The *Daily Times,* in its editorial of March 11, 1959, remarked that "the new TUC must look into the past and learn from the pitfalls of its predecessor, the old TUC" under Nduka Eze.[99] In the final analysis, the constitution of the new TUC categorically stated as one of the objectives of the new labour movement "it will safeguard against the projection of communism into the labor movement."[100]

THE ROLE OF MAJOR POLITICAL PARTIES

Ideological questions did not emerge in party politics and the wider nationalist movement in Nigeria until 1944, when the National Council of Nigeria and the Cameroons was formed. Although the Marxists were unable to make NCNC a Communist-oriented organization, its efforts, thenceforth, were aimed at achieving strategic positions within the party. To the NCNC, a Communist Party of Nigeria that preached violence had no right to exist. The party opted for gradualism and a constitutional route to independence, in opposition to the radicals' idea of violent liberation.[101]

In addition, the Action Group and the Northern People's Congress were anti-Communist in orientation and structure. This, perhaps, was based upon their significant support from traditional institutions. Both the AG and the NPC first emerged as cultural associations called "Egbe Omo Oduduwa" and "Jamatul Islamiyyah Arewa," respectively, in the late 1940s. They, however, became political parties in 1951. To the Marxists, both parties were conservative and could not serve their purpose (a base for militant leftist action). However, this view about the Action Group later changed in the 1960s. By and large, the AG and NPC membership was made up of politicians who had been schooled in the virtues of capitalism and communism. While most opted for capitalism and Fabian socialism, some who had earlier been associated with the CPGB in London, renounced communism upon returning to Nigeria. These were barristers, businessmen, teachers, and aristocrats. Both parties were manifestly interested in anti-leftist ideology as part of the decolonization process.

In view of the government's stiff opposition to leftist organizations, some of the Marxists (Eze group) had, by the mid-1950s, decided to join registered political parties. There was, however, a dilemma among the Marxist groups concerning which of the political parties they should join. A majority of them, however, preferred the Action Group. Sklar identified four reasons for this. First, the Left had recently suffered setbacks due to Azikiwe's anti-Communism; second, they were impressed by the organization and methodical planning of the Action Group; Third, their membership was concentrated in the West; and fourth, they preferred AG's federalism to the NCNC's preference for a unitary system.[102] They were also attracted to the Action Group because of its soft spot for socialist intellectuals, whom it used in its "summer school" programs. The AG used the "summer school" to teach party aims, activities, and strategies. Thus between 1952 and 1960 the Action Group repeatedly made known its preference for free enterprise and welfarism. To Awolowo, these included free education, health services, full employment and unemployment relief, as well as support and encouragement of peasant farmers.[103]

Ideological questions in the North are better understood by explaining the attitude of the NPC to opposition parties such as the Northern Elements People's Party (NEPU) and other minorities. The NPC leadership under Ahmadu Bello did not mince words in its stiff opposition to leftist ideology and its micro-organizations in Nigeria.[104] This explains his attitude toward socialists and radicals in the Northern Region during the period. Examples of radicalism include opposition to the native authority system in any form. An example of socialist ideology includes NEPU's declared principle of resuscitating the role of the "Talakawa" in politics. In fact, the North's native authority was the NPC and vice versa. Thus, opposition to the NA system meant opposition to the NPC. Aminu Kano perceptively summed up the situation thus: "We interpret democracy in its more traditional, radical sense, and that is the rule of the common people, the poor, the illiterate, while our opponents (the NPC) interpret it in its modern Tory sense, and that is the rule of the enlightened and prosperous minority in the supposed interest of the common people."[105]

Aminu Kano's position, according to Dudley, "provided the middle-class led opposition with a radical, revolutionary ideology which drew its inspiration from Marxian concepts."[106] Unlike Marxists in the South, the NEPU under Kano aimed at restructuring the fabric of Northern society and propagated the need for wider political and economic opportunities based upon meritocracy rather than ascription.[107] Dudley described NEPU's ideology as "the building up of the economy on socialist lines, which the party interprets to mean the conversion of villages into co-operatives and the gradual nationalization of some assets."[108] The NPC, like the NCNC, did not tolerate socialism and any opposition to aristocracy preached by NEPU and other minority groups in the North.[109] As it was in the South, there was no place for the Marxists in the North. Unlike the southern parties, however, the NPC did not accept radicals into its fold even if they were willing to shed their "red garments."[110]

CONCLUSION

By the late 1950s, Britain, with the assistance of leading Nigerian politicians, had been able to stall the development of a nationwide Marxist organization in Nigeria. It also established practical policies on sociopolitical and economic development as well. It succeeded in winning the hearts and souls of many Nigerians, as in most of its colonies before granting independence. More importantly, it laid the foundation for sustaining measures and policies used in preventing Leftists in-road into public and private sectors in Nigeria. Emergent leaders in a post-independent Nigeria were also anti-leftist a-la Westminster in all ramifications. Thus the continuation of a pro-Western structure, ideals, and anti-leftist measures should not be surprising.

Chapter Seven

The United States, France, and the Nigerian Marxists

INTRODUCTION

Recent studies about Cold War politics in colonial dependencies fill a critical lacuna in the literature, as scholars had been slow to recognize the important economic and strategic position of particular colonial dependencies during the era of US-Soviet bipolarity.[1] So too, there is a continuing need for many more serious studies about the role of non-governing powers in colonial territories during the transition to independence, although the nature and availability of official and private papers make the venture an enterprising one. Intelligence, political, and consular agents at the time well recognized the strategic position of key colonial dependencies (their ports, airfields and natural resources) and viewed with alarm the communist infiltration of indigenous nationalist politics.

This chapter analyses the role of the United States in Nigeria, Britain's most populous and vibrant colony, with particular emphasis on the role of the U.S. Consulate and the United States Information Service in Nigeria during the 1950s. We have identified three main reasons for firm U.S. support of British anti-leftist policies in Nigeria during the period under study. These are

(1) Identification of Marxist groups in Nigeria after the World War II.
(2) An increase in shipment of Marxist literature from Cominform and Communist Party of Great Britain (CPGB).
(3) Cominform and communist fronts' funds to notable leftists.

Since the U.S. was not the only ally, a section is devoted to collaborations with the neighboring French colonial government as well.

THE BACKGROUND: LEFTISTS IN THE UNITED STATES

Across the Atlantic, Americans were profoundly affected by Communist bogey and subsequent government anti-Communism. The root of this phenomenon was the Red Scare of 1919–1920, leftist momentum in intellectual circles, and labor militancy in the United States. The forerunners of anti-Communism in the United States were the National Chamber of Commerce, the Federal Bureau of Investigation (FBI), the press, and the Catholic Church. The chamber blamed leftists for post-war militancy and sought the assistance of the FBI to quell it. Both conservative and liberal media was used to disrupt the activities of the leftist groups as well during the period. By the same token, the Catholic Church disliked Communism partly because of its exponents' persecution of Catholics in Eastern Europe. The Department of State was also at the forefront of anti-Communist policies with Dean Acheson formulating and directing Cold War policies and foreign affairs. He was not only influential but was the brain behind most of Truman's executive orders and policies against Communists within the government.[2]

In 1947, President Harry Truman set the ball rolling against Communists and leftist organizations within the United States by issuing an Executive Order 9835 on loyalty and security. The Order required the Department of Justice to draw up a list of organizations it decided were totalitarian, fascist, communist or subversive; or those seeking to alter the form of government of the United States by unconstitutional means.[3] It emphasized, for clarity purposes it seems, not only membership in, but also "sympathetic association" with, any organization on the Attorney General's list would be considered in determining disloyalty.

Senator Joseph McCarthy and his group were also bent on getting rid of communists imagined or real in all sectors of the society. Suspected leftists or sympathizers were either not given employment or had their appointment terminated. The government, it seems, was interested in winning the battle for the souls of men by getting rid of leftist professors in publicly funded colleges and universities.[4] Blacks were particularly targeted because of their militant activism and opposition to the government's inability to address the deteriorating race relations during the period.

For instance, in 1954 the "The House Un-American Activities Committee" (HUAC) denounced the National Labor Conference for Negro Rights and the National Negro Labor Councils and branded them as communist fronts. And by 1956 these organizations enjoyed at best, a suspended animation. When W. E. B. Du Bois, a prominent African American in the first half of the twentieth century, ran for a New York senate seat in 1950, he was indicted as a foreign agent. Du Bois, one of the first American sociologists, author of numerous books, editor of *The Crisis* from 1910 to 1934, was at the time a socialist. Although he was eighty-two, President Harry S. Truman had him handcuffed and displayed to the media as a criminal. Charges against Du Bois were dismissed for lack of evidence in 1951, but his passport was nonetheless revoked.

The State Department also revoked the passport of internationally famous black singer and actor Paul Robeson, denying him access to the concerts he had booked around the world, concerts that supplied his considerable income. However, Robeson was never charged with an illegal action, arrested, nor tried.

The climax was a speech given by McCarthy at a Women's Republican Club in Wheeling, West Virginia, in 1950. Addressing the women, he shouted: "I have here in my hand a list of 205—a list of names that were made known to the Secretary of State as being members of the Communist Party and who nevertheless are still working and shaping policy in the State Department." A few months afterwards, he contradicted himself while speaking in Salt Lake City, on the number of supposed Communists in the State Department. He put the figure at fifty-seven. And when he spoke on the floor of the Senate he claimed the total number to be a hundred. Needless to say, McCarthy spiced the evidence to suit his main goal of depriving Communists and leftist groups any space within the society.

McCarthy's momentum seems to have been influenced by a bipartisan approval of "McCarran Act or Internal Security Act" in 1950 that required the registration of organizations found to be "Communist-action" or "Communist-front." Even liberal Senators did not fight that head-on. Instead, some of them, including Hubert Humphrey and Herbert Lehman, proposed a substitute measure: the setting up of detention centers or concentration camps for suspected subversives, who, when the President declared an "internal security emergency," would be held without trial. The detention-camp bill became not a substitute for, but an addition to, the Internal Security Act, and the proposed camps were set up, ready for use. In fact, the Immigration and Naturalization Service detained foreign nationals known to be Communists or leftist sympathizers without bail pending deportation hearings during the period.

Another important piece of legislation was soon added in 1954 when the Communist Control Act was passed. The background was McCarthy's role as chairman of the Permanent Investigations Sub-Committee of a Senate

Committee on Government Operations. The Sub-Committee investigated the State Department's information program, its Voice of America, and its overseas libraries, which included books by peoples, McCarthy considered Communists. He soon met a waterloo in the spring of 1954 when he began hearings to investigate supposed subversives in the military. His attack on military generals as being Communists or sympathizers did not go down well with the bipartisan Congress. And in December 1954, the Senate voted overwhelmingly to censure him for "conduct . . . unbecoming of a Member of the United States Senate." The censure resolution, however, avoided criticism of McCarthy's anti-Communist tactics, lies, and exaggerations. The U.S. Congress complemented this by passing a whole series of anti-Communist bills. Hubert Humphrey introduced an amendment to one of the bills to make the Communist party illegal in both continental United States and its overseas possessions. The most important bill was the Communist Control Act of 1954.

Despite McCarthy's shortcoming, liberal and conservative politicians were resolved to brow beat Communists and all forms of Leftism in the United States. The following excerpts from the legislation "Communist Control Act of 1954," clarifies U.S. resolve at dealing with Communists and their sympathizers within:

In determining membership or participation in the Communist party of or in any other organization defined in this act, or knowledge of the purpose or objective of such party or organization, the jury, under instructions from the court, shall consider evidence, if presented, as to whether the accused person . . . Has written, spoken, or in any other way communicated by signal, semaphore, sign, or in any other form of communication, orders, directives, or plans of the organization . . . Has indicated by word, action, conduct, writing, or in any other way a willingness to carry out in any manner and to any degree the plans, designs, objectives, or purposes of the organization; Has in any other way participated in the activities, planning, actions, objectives, or purposes of the organization.

It should be stressed that out of the 150 people charged with leftist membership or sympathy, only two (Julius and Ethel Rosenberg) were convicted for treason and espionage during the period. The "Venona" files released by the National Security Archive in July 1995 indicate that there were indeed communist sympathizers in the State Department and other high places.[5]

THE NIGERIAN CONTEXT

Louis Johnson, the Secretary for Defense in 1949, formulated the basis of American collaboration with colonial powers' anti-leftist policies and worldwide anti-Communism. In a memorandum to the National Security Council in June 1949, Johnson stated thus:

(a) "Cooperate locally with security organisations to combat Communist subversive activities to the extent that this can be done without assisting in the repression of responsible non-Communist nationalist movements";

(b) "Seek to prevent or at least curtail formal representation of Sino-Soviet bloc countries in Africa;"

(c) "Seek to provide constructive alternatives to Soviet blandishments but avoid trying to compete with every Soviet offer;"

(d) "Give general support to non-Communist nationalists, and reform movements, balancing the nature and degree of such support, however, with consideration of (our) NATO allies"; and,

(e) "In areas where trade unionism develops, guide it towards Western models by working with the International Confederation of Free Trade Unions, by direct advice and assistance, and by an exchange of persons program."[6]

To Johnson, a major objective of U.S. policy was to contain leftist ideology in order to reduce its threat to U.S. and allies security. This was the guide for consular and intelligence officers researching and documenting leftist activities, nationalism, economic and strategic potentials of the colonies, capabilities of the Soviet Union and her changing tactics towards the colonies, conducted throughout the period.

United States officials in Lagos and other parts of West Africa identified four principal phases of communist penetration during the period under review. Stage one saw communist party member recruitment efforts among Nigerian students in the United Kingdom, followed up by indoctrination and training either by the CPGB itself, or in a university in the Soviet bloc, such as the University of Prague. Stage two involved concerted infiltration and control of nascent Nigerian labor movements, focusing particular attention on The All-Nigerian Trade Union Federation (ANTUF); the agenda called for pushing such groups to obtain WFTU affiliation, while at the same time pushing them away from ICFTU and British trade union influence. The third phase relied upon the distribution of propaganda, primarily printed matter, through direct mail or a certain small chain of bookshops in major southern Nigerian cities. Finally, stage four, turned upon efforts to place expatriate party members in influential official positions in the Nigerian civil service, or on the staff of the University College, Ibadan, and in the quasi-official department of Extra-Mural Studies.

In early 1951, A. W. Childs, the U.S. Consular General in Nigeria, advised that the United States must render support to the governing authorities should the home country be unable to provide for internal security. By the same token, Anglo-American officials at the United Nations agreed that nothing should be done at the UN to delay the achievement of self-government by colonies. The U.S. position was to support liberal nationalists, encourage policies and actions of colonial powers that lead to self-government, and avoid identifying with metropolitan policies considered stagnant or repressive.[7]

The background to this was the growing and intensified Marxian nationalism in Nigeria that threatened the colonial power and Special Force/Police report of a sabotage plan by the Marxists.[8] Nothing intensified Anglo-American interest in the colonies more than the fear of the possible spread of Communism. Organizing the colonies against leftist ideology before independence (and afterwards) was an important aspect of the transition that the United States strongly supported.

Between 1948 and 1960, both the U.S. and Britain shared the desire to deny the African continent to Communists. The United States defined its position in Africa in terms of the Cold War and Communist threats, though nothing like the Marshall Plan was envisaged.[9] In fact, the American public and Congressmen were more responsive to issues of anti-Communist sentiments and mutual security than any other matter. As Henry Kissinger noted some decades afterwards, "The United States possessed the full panoply of the means—political, economic, and military—to organize the defence of the non-communist World."[10] It was in the national interest of the United States for Africa to be free of Communism that motivated support for British anti-left policies.

The historical antecedent was the change from a policy of isolationism to containment. World War II changed the United States' global position, as it emerged as a super power. Immediate post-war American policy aimed at preventing Communist in-roads into developed economies and colonial dependencies (in collaboration with the governing power). Perhaps, the most significant intelligence report during the Truman era was the *"Report on the Strategic Ports of West Africa."* This was an attempt by the U.S. National Security Resources Board to evaluate and observe firsthand, political, economic and particularly port security situations and problems as they might affect the national security interests of the United States in the event of mobilization for total war, whether in the immediate future or over the longer term. The report recommended that, West Africa must be preserved by Britain as her colonial master, as an integral part of the Free World.

The strategic location of Nigeria, its population, critical raw materials, and its potentialities as an industrial and military supply centre made it important in United States' anti-leftist policy.

In fact, Nigeria played a momentary prominent role between 1940 and 1941 when it became the only line of communication by air to the Middle East and the Far East due to the closure of the Mediterranean. During this period, an important part of the United States' air effort largely depended on Nigerian bases. British African colonies alone contributed 374,000 troops to the Allies.[11] U.S. officials reinforced Africa's strategic position and its significance in global security in the 1950s. The overall goal was to encourage colonial power to provide structure, both human and non-human, against onslaught of leftist ideology.

There was also an economic reason for United States' support for anti-leftist policy in Africa. Contrary to Andrew Kamarck, the United States had economic interest in Africa during and after World War II.[12] Its interests can be divided into direct and indirect. The direct interest was based on the abundant labor and untapped natural resources in Africa. To the United States, West Africa was a strategic storehouse for American industry because of its resources. Contrary to existing views, the United States did not see West Africa as a foreign policy "backwater" and of "lowest priority." Rather it saw the area as significant in terms of collaborative exploitation of its untapped resources. The United States was dependent on West Africa, particularly Ghana and Nigeria, "for nearly all of our cobalt requirements, nearly all of our columbium, most of our palm oil, most of the critical bolt type of industrial diamonds, over half of our tantalum, a growing proportion of our manganese and an appreciable amount of our tin."[13] An official concluded as early as 1952 that "West Africa is the largest source of uranium in the world and most of the output comes to the United States. The national security of the United States and the fate of West Africa are closely interrelated."[14]

This conclusion should not be surprising because the United States (as well as Britain) depended on Nigeria's palm kernels, palm oil, tin ores, rubber, columbium ore, wolfram and potash during the 1950s. Seventy-three percent of the total imports of columbium ore into the United States in 1950 were obtained from Nigeria. Columbium ore exports reached 1,092 tons in 1951, which represented an increase of 51 long tons over 1950. Also, in 1950, seventeen percent of palm oil imported into the United States came from Nigeria. Although most of Nigeria's rubber was exported to Britain, the United States remained the second largest importer of rubber from Nigeria during the 1950s.

The United States indirect interest was also intertwined with its strategic interest in Europe as the main battleground against the Soviet bloc. As McKay put it at the time, "it is an economic interest in Europe which is affected by Africa's economic relations with Europe."[15] Certainly, one must look beyond official U.S. programs, given traditional American reliance upon private initiatives and free enterprise. The U.S. government encouraged (though covertly) private organizations to work with African entrepreneurs in the development of the economy. In West Africa, the Rockefeller Brothers West African Fund was set up in 1957 to research and document feasibility studies about resources in the territory. Such studies served as the data bank for local and foreign investors during the transition to independence and after.[16]

A sound economic development before independence was linked with political and educational progress in the colonies. The United States encouraged Britain to continue with its decolonization plans as a basis for a special relationship with the Nigerian leaders. Both liberal political and labor leaders were sponsored, encouraged, and supported in their efforts against Marxist groups.[17] There is no doubt that the educated elites were of high priority because they personified the worst fears of the Anglo-American imagination regarding the nature of anti-colonial protest and attempts by Marxist groups to make in-roads into labor and nationalist politics during the decolonization years.[18]

The U.S. Department of State noted in 1946 that "it is thought that the eyes of certain of the more vociferous African exponents of early political independence have turned toward USSR because of what they considered to be [the] Soviet Union's advanced attitude toward dependent people."[19] There was anxiety that the Soviet bloc could benefit from anti-colonial sentiments in the colonies if the metropolitan government did not take initiative.[20]

THE NEW ERA

A new era began at the Department of State when Elmer Bourgerie was appointed as the director of African Affairs in 1950. With the assistance of George McGhee and the U.S. consulate in Lagos, United States' interest in colonial Nigeria was given more attention. Bourgerie's secret official directives to Childs (Consul General) remain the most useful evidence for assessing the U.S. position on Marxist activities in Nigeria during the 1950s. Childs was specifically directed to keep the Department of State informed on general conditions in Nigeria. To Bourgerie "our immediate and long-range policy is how may we perpetuate this fundamental relationship and prevent any deterioration thereof which would lead to a conflict between African peoples and the Free World, be it ideological or philosophical."[21]

This view is fundamental to Childs and his staff in Nigeria because it formed the basis for all related intelligence (political and economic) reports. It was recognized that anti-colonial feelings in Nigeria constituted a formidable problem for the Free World. American officials insisted that Britain must exert greater efforts to forge links with Nigerian liberals. Childs and his staff were directed to encourage both British officials and Nigerian nationalists (whenever the opportunity arose) that "the road to survival is one of well-balanced economic and political development with emphasis on the right privileges which the Soviets have exploited so successfully in other World areas."[22]

Furthermore, analyses of Nigerian political conditions by U.S. consulate in Lagos focused on the political mood of the urban and rural African; the description of local parties and movements, with biographic sketches and appraisals of leaders; and finally, the identification and categorization of subversive individuals, organizations, or movements. An assessment of Nigeria's economic potential included estimates of mineral resources, timber resources, industrial capacity, agricultural development, hydro-electric development, and transport facilities. On the social side, the American focus was on urbanization, detribalization and assimilation by Nigerians of western values. Also important was the imperative to discern and report any Soviet influence on native or European groups.[23]

In late 1951, Childs forwarded *The Political, Economic and Social Survey of Nigeria* to Bourgerie.[24] In the report, Childs described the political situation and regrouping of the Marxists under a different umbrella. Analysis of efforts by governing authorities was described with the highest praise reserved for initiatives against leftist nationalism. Childs recommended that political appointments should be made with an eye toward persuading nationalists and encouraging more collaboration. As he states: "Given the very high ambition of the great majority of the political leaders in Nigeria for both political prestige and monetary gain, the government will probably be able to control a number of these firebrands through its influence in the choice of officials."[25]

There were, however, some officials who believed that the British were moving far too fast toward decolonization, thus unwittingly instigating the chaos so hospitable to radicalism. To this group, Nigeria in the early 1950s was not ripe for self-government. Bartelt was of the opinion that "a rapidly increasing measure of self-government is been given to an African people who are very vague about what it is."[26] The argument was that British decolonization was too rapid for sustained anti-Marxist measures.

There was a common ground among US officials based on the need to train Nigerians in labor management and the Foreign Service. Toward these ends, labor leaders were trained in the United States and Britain, and then were given support against Marxist labor leaders.[27] Some were sent to ICFTU labor training school at Kampala, Uganda, to learn trade unionism and a western way of life. By October of 1958, the ICFTU had purchased a building at Ebute-Metta, Lagos, which served as the office for ICFTU representative and a training centre.

It was through the ICFTU office in Lagos that various measures were taken against Marxist labor leaders. The office served as a think-tank for the ICFTU, the International Cooperation Administration (ICA), the AFL-CIO and the Nigeria Department of Labour throughout the 1950s.[28] ICA workers' education kits were forwarded to Nigeria Department of Labour on a regular basis, for use by trade union education officers in each region. The US Department of Labor in Washington D.C. also sent academic materials and books through the USIS for use at the centre. Also included were publications from AFL-CIO and NATO, which focused on guidance for labor-management relations, question and answers on American labor, and ongoing world affairs.[29]

The background to these activities was the discovery that radical groups were sending funds to Marxist labor leaders in Nigeria.[30] The World Federation of Trade Unions (WFTU) was able to send funds to Nigeria through Dr. Felix Roland Moumie, the leader of the United Peoples Congress (UPC) of the French Cameroon. Communist literature was also channeled through him to ANTUF. Funds and literature continued to come through Moumie and his network even after his deportation to Khartoum, Sudan. An intelligence report by the Central Intelligence Department (CID) Division of the Nigeria Police indicates that Moumie often sent funds through an unnamed French African physician in Dahomey, where they were brought by agents aboard vessels or by land and picked up in Nigeria, not by union members, but by one or two Lagos attorneys—V. Okafor or O. Ekineh.[31] It was through these men that Amaefula Ikoro, G. Nzeribe, and E.A. Cowan were able to get funds for Marxist activities during the 1950s.[32]

Nigeria also benefited from U.S. Point IV program instituted by Truman administration in 1950. This was a technical assistance program passed by the United States Congress in September 1950 to assist its European allies in developing their colonies. A section is devoted to this economic exploitation through the Economic Cooperation Act [ECA](1950) and the Mutual Security Act [MSA](1951) respectively. Of significance under the Point IV program is the training of Nigerian Foreign Service Officer Cadre in 1957 by

U.S. Department of State. Under an arrangement with the British, the first batch of forty Nigerian diplomats began training in Washington D.C. under the supervision of Reginald Barrett. Another batch of six Nigerians was sent to Washington D.C. with their wives to learn diplomacy, ethics, and the essence of western values. These were the first assistant secretaries in the Nigeria Federal department of External Affairs. While in the United States, the trainees were attached to the British Embassy and Department of State where they learned diplomacy and acquired practical experience. They also observed the United Nation's proceeding as British delegates during their study in the United States. Academic lectures were attended at the School of Advanced International Studies, Johns Hopkins University in Maryland.[33]

The battle for the souls and hearts of colonial people was important to Western powers. It was important to officials that local leaders must be persuaded to think and act as "models" for western views. This is partly the basis for US leadership program inaugurated in 1947. Nominations were made in Nigeria, as in other parts of the colonial world, based upon identification and recommendation by colonial officials to U.S. consul of colonials worthy of investing on. The program exposed selected individuals to U.S. culture, ethics, and international perception; selected individuals visited and participated in a "mind bending" program in Washington D.C. and its environ. Upon returning to Nigeria these individuals were expected to keep close ties with U.S. officials and remain goodwill ambassadors of U.S. goals and ideals. It should not be surprising that many Nigerians in key positions that cut across labor, welfare, education, cultural organisation, and native authority were selected for the leadership program.

THE ROLE OF THE UNITED STATES INFORMATION SERVICE

The United States Information Service (Agency) like the British Council served as the vanguard against misinformation by the Communists during the Cold War. The Agency's role in colonial Nigeria, however, remained a footnote in the US-British relationship. The forerunner of the USIS was United States Information and Educational Exchange Act (USIEEA) of 1948, also known as the Smith-Mundt Act. With the onset of the Cold War, it became natural that an information, if not also a propaganda, agency was needed to disseminate the ideas of the people and government of the United States, as against the disinformation spread by rivals. In 1953, Eisenhower changed and refined the USIEEA to USIS, charging the Agency to "submit evidence to peoples of other nations by means of communication technique that, the objectives and policy of the United States are in harmony with, and will advance their legitimate aspirations of freedom, progress and peace."[34]

The Agency first operated within the Consulate Office in Lagos until 1953. The first office of the Agency was opened in 1953, with Enugu and Kaduna following in 1954. Agency officials worked closely with Nigeria Public Relations Department and the British Council in Lagos throughout the 1950s. For instance, local administration in Nigeria sought the assistance of the USIS in 1950 as part of collaboration against increasing Communist literature, a ban on the Zikist movement, and a ban on the employment of Communists in public and private sectors.[35] Throughout the transition period in Nigeria, the USIS implemented pro-western propaganda disseminated information through the *"Labour Bulletin,"* and also acted as the liaison between liberal nationalists and the ICFTU and AFL-CIO. The Agency published counter propaganda leaflets and pamphlets and published a newsletter. Radio communication was broadcast through the Voice of America to the Nigerian public.[36]

The growing significance of the USIS in African areas was evident in the increase in number of officials sent to Nigeria in the late 1950s. For instance, seven out of the twenty Foreign Officers posted to Nigeria on the eve of independence were assigned to USIS. And by 1961, the three regional governments had been assigned a USIS officer (the North was assigned two). The Agency emphasized education and scholarship as the means to win the hearts and minds of young Nigerians. It facilitated scholarship awards/grants to Nigerians for research purposes. A few months before independence in October 1960, twenty-four Nigerians were granted scholarships under the auspices of African Scholarship Program of American Universities (ASPAU) to study different courses in the United States.[37] And by 1961, the senior and junior Fulbright academic award had been instituted with USIS as the sole facilitator.

DEVELOPMENT OR ECONOMIC EXPLOITATION?

Records in England and the United States point to the fact that the basis of U.S. government interest in Africa during the colonial period (and afterwards) was economic exploitation of the abundant resources. Leading officials did not hide the need for exploitation of the untapped natural resources useful in technological and scientific undertakings in the United States and Britain. In 1950 for instance, it was realized that Nigeria supplied ninety five percent of world's columbium. This is a metal derived from tin ore used for armaments and industrial projects. The resource is also useful in the manufacture of gas turbines, jet engine components, as carbide stabilizer in stainless steels, in electrodes for stainless steels, alloys, and chemical equipments.[38]

The question is how did the quest for exploitation of the vital reservoir of minerals and natural resources that are critical stockpile items in the United States during the colonial era pursued? Collaboration with the colonial powers (British and French) through treaties and trade agreements were some of the ways exploitation was carried out.

But first, I will address the collaborative efforts of the United States and the colonial powers in West Africa with emphasis on Nigeria. It began in July 1946 when talks were held between British and United States officials in London. Officials agreed upon an economic cooperation between the two partners with a view to further develop their thought. The views about economic cooperation were amended by exchanges of "notes" between officials on January 3, 1950. And on January 27, 1950, the two governments signed an Economic Cooperation Agreement at Washington D.C. on January 27, 1950. This was not only approved by the U.S. Congress but was followed by another agreement, the Mutual Security Act of May 25, 1951 also approved by the Congress under Public Law 165, 82nd Congress. The Mutual Security Act of 1951 was an amendment to the Mutual Defence Assistance Act of 1949 between Great Britain and the United States.

The centrality of both agreements as they relate to British West Africa is US strategic interest in procuring raw materials, partly as a result of the outbreak of the Korean War in June 1950 and as part of the covert measures taken during the Cold War period in general. As Oliver Lyttleton, the Secretary of State for the colonies noted, "the primary importance of strengthening the mutual security and individual and collective defences of the free world."[39]

He stated further that "developing their resources in the interest of the security and independence and national interest of friendly countries and facilitating the effective participation of those countries . . . for collective security."[40] John Orchard, chairman of the ECA Advisory Committee, better summarized the exploitative nature of the Economic Cooperation Agreement. To him the ECA was to support European recovery and to ensure the possibilities of increasing raw material production, including strategic materials for the United States stockpile.[41] The same view was aired by Allan Smith, the acting director of the Overseas Territories Division of the ECA in 1951. Smith was of the opinion that "dependent overseas territories have generally been considered by ECA as appendages of European economy or as producers of strategic materials for the U.S. stockpile."[42]

To Her Majesty's government, economic cooperation and other bilateral agreements with the United States was based on six pedestals:

(a) Join in promoting international understanding and goodwill, and maintaining world peace;

(b) Take such action as may be mutually agreed upon to eliminate causes of international tension;

(c) Fulfill the military obligations which they have assumed under multilateral or bilateral agreements or treaties to which the United States is a party;

(d) Make, consistent with their political and economic stability, the full contribution, permitted by their manpower, resources, facilities, and general economic condition, to the development and maintenance of their own defensive strength and the defensive strength of the free world;

(e) Take all reasonable measures which may be needed to develop their defence capacities;

(f) Take appropriate steps to insure the effective utilization of the economic and military assistance provided by the United States.[43]

It should not be surprising that the two governments established effective procedures suitable for exploitation of vital resources in the colonies based on their mutual agreement under the ECA and MSA respectively. Largely, whatever human or capital projects carried out were based on selfish interest. Apart from the fact that the colonies indirectly paid for projects carried out with their vital resources, measures were put in place to protect British and the United States finances. For instance, Article IV of ECA stipulated among others that:

(a) Expenditures of sums allocated to the use of the Government of the United States pursuant to paragraph 4 of article IV of the Economic Cooperation Agreement will not be limited to expenditures in the United Kingdom.

(b) The government of the United kingdom will so deposit, segregate or protect their title to all funds allocated to them or derived by them from any program of assistance undertaken by the Government of the United States that such funds shall not be subject to garnishee proceedings, attachment, seizure or other legal process by any person, firm, agency, corporation, organization or government.

(c) Pounds Sterling will be deposited pursuant to Article IV of the Economic Cooperation Agreement commensurate with assistance on a grant basis in the form of transfers of funds pursuant to Section III (*d*) of the Economic Cooperation Act of 1948, in the way as amounts commensurate with the dollar cost commodities, services and technical assistance are deposited pursuant to that Article.[44]

The United States went a step further in its scheme to benefit from the economic cooperation and mutual security agreement as it related to the colonies exports. It requested a tax exemption from "common defence effort and for aid programmes."[45] On their side, the British willingly agreed to facilitate such exemption whenever requested. To British officials the exemption should be seen as a relief rather than direct refunds to the government of the United States. Delegates from the "Special United States Tax Delegation" were assured by the colonial office that at the request of the Government of the United States, it would consult with the authorities of the dependent overseas territory concerned regarding the possibility of obtaining for the government of the United States appropriate relief or exemption similar to the obtained in the United Kingdom.[46] That aside it was also agreed that quarterly reports about projects carried out must be given to United States controlled Mutual Security Agency via the Secretary of State for the colonies in London.

In Nigeria as elsewhere in British colonies, such projects were classified as "Overseas Development Pool." The most significant projects undertaken during the 1950s was the development of the Enugu Colliery and the construction of a road from Kano to Fort Lamy via Maiduguri under the Overseas Development Pool fund. The background to this is not far fetched. Enugu Colliery had been a centre of discontent among labor unionists in late 1940s. The report of the government panel that looked into the uprising that took place in 1949 had indicated a need to improve the working conditions, among other issues, of the employees within the area. Established by Ordinance No. 29 of 1950 the Nigerian Coal Corporation engaged in coal exploration, exploitation, and marketing. The Enugu Colliery was transferred from the Railway Corporation to the NCC and its reconstruction fell under the ODP. With a population of 63,000[47] in 1953, Enugu was not only becoming a vibrant urban centre but also an important labor and nationalist meeting point outside Lagos.

Out of the £365,000 and £162,000 spent on Kano-Fort Lamy road and the Enugu Colliery under the Development Pool Scheme in 1950/1951, £31,910 and £13,650 were considered grants by the United States government. As stated earlier different colonies adopted different format in executing aid under the US ECA (which by September 1952 had been solely an MSA affair). When the projects were approved in August 1951, the administering officer in Nigeria, working with the director of audit, inspector-general of public works, director of commerce and industries, and chairman Nigerian Coal Corporation, was given directives toward realizing the completion of the projects in a timely manner.

Since the ECA was prevented by legislation from making direct grants from ODP to finance the non-dollar content of projects, the colonial government and Colonial Office worked out a formula that would benefit both the Motherland and the United States. The following procedure was adopted:

(a) Nigerian importers of America wheat-flour and tobacco, when importing these commodities with dollars received through the medium of the Nigerian Exchange Control by import licenses in the normal way quote a special Procurement Authorization (P.A.) No; supplied to them by the ECA through the Secretary of State and the Director of Commerce and Industries, on all documents and correspondence with the U.S. supplier.

(b) The American supplier then forwards to the United Kingdom Treasury and Supply Delegation in Washington certain documents indicating the value of the dollar exports of wheat-flour and tobacco made to the Nigerian buyers.

(c) The U.K. Treasury and Supply Delegation then claims on an E.C.A. a refund of the dollars expended by Nigerian importers. This being made, an equivalent amount in sterling is paid by the United Kingdom Government into a special account at the Bank of England. Thereafter the Crown Agents are authorized to make grants up to the sterling equivalent of the ECA contribution towards the approved projects.[48]

Payment to the Crown Agents was subject to a quarterly satisfactory report from the inspector-general of public works (for Kano-Lamy road) and chairman of the Nigerian Coal Corporation (Enugu Colliery).[49] A final technical and financial report was also sent through the Secretary of State for the colonies to the MSA on every project.

FRANCE: A NEIGHBOR AND COLONIAL POWER

One of the policies supported by the Colonial Office was the encouragement of a closer relation with its western allies i.e. United States and France. Unlike the United States, the French were both a neighboring colonial power and a western ally. The French government had to deal with the French Communist Party in France and in the colonies. Like their British counterpart, the French government took measures to curtail the French

Communist Party's activities among the colonial people. In West Africa, it collaborated with British administration in depriving west coast of Africa to the leftist groups and their sponsors. This collaboration is conceptualized as the "Third World Power."

Between 1951 and 1960 there were attempts towards improving upon Ernest Bevin's idea of a "Third World Power." The idea of a "Third World Power" was consummated in 1949 when Bevin, as the Secretary of State for Foreign Affairs, suggested closer ties with colonial and non-colonial powers within the western bloc.[50] The purpose was to consolidate the gains of the Western world in the colonies against International Communism led by the Soviet Union.

Despite differences of emphasis, Anglo-French views about anti-leftist strategies recognized and accepted the reality of the Soviet Union's political interest, financial and moral support of Marxist and radical groups in the colonies (and at the United Nations Assembly and Security Council meetings). While France was concerned more with diagnosing the situation in her colonies in West and North Africa, Madagascar and South-east Asia, British officials were skeptical about the secrecy of Anglo-French talks on Communism as the French Communist Party remained a strong political force in government (1946–1947) and outside the government.

As a Foreign Office report highlighted, "Anglo-French talks on Communism were a poor security risk as agreement reached might become known to the French Communist Party" in the long run (although the French Communist Party had ceased since 1947 to be part of the government, this did not avert fear among some senior British officials).[51]

Despite such skepticism, officials of the Foreign Office and the *Quai d'Orsay* met to discuss international aspects of the situation. To the French, the colonies had to be economically self-sufficient before independence so as to shield them from Soviet Union economic aid. There were meetings, talks, and exchanges of correspondence between British and French officials about policies in their West African colonies throughout the period. One should note that discussions, however, transcended Communism and anti-Communism. Issues such as the Ewe unification and technical, economic cooperation, development of the colonial resources, and intelligence were also encouraged.[52]

As far back as 1945, Anglo-French technical co-operation had developed. Conferences covering the West African region, or the whole of Africa south of the Sahara, were held on many technical subjects. Officials noted that: "Useful contacts have been established and valuable practical recommendations have emerged."[53]

In 1948, closer co-operation in the economic sphere was agreed upon. More important was the agreement in June 1948 between Britain and France about exchange of information and the development of closer contacts both in Europe and West Africa. Part of the agreement was that Information should be exchanged between the two Governments and between the local administrations over a wide range of constitutional, local government and other political questions; that Studies Branches should be maintained in the two Colonial Ministries; that contacts should be developed at all levels between the territories in West Africa; and that for this purpose not exchanges of visits but exchanges of postings should take place.[54]

At another meeting in May 1949, Britain proposed an Anglo-French Secretariat to be based at Accra to "promote co-operation and exchange of information."[55] One can say that Anglo-French relations were largely cordial in West Africa. There was frequent exchange visits between Governors and senior officials "and some very valuable discussions on matters of common interest."[56]

By August 1950, senior officials met regularly; and some District officers were said to have met on a day-to-day basis. Perhaps the greatest efforts as it relates to Anglo-French exchange of information were Harry Cooper's (Head, Public Relations Department, Nigeria) visit to Dakar in 1950. The outcome was a comprehensive program of co-operation between the various information units in the French and British colonies. The governments also exchanged official bulletins and other publications as they related to administration of their colonies and the trend of political agitations.[57]

CONCLUSION

The potentiality of subversion by Marxist groups in Nigeria made the pursuit of anti-Marxist measures (by Britain) inevitable. United States support of these measures was based partly on its role as the leader of the Western-bloc and its resolve to exploit the vital natural resources abundant in Africa. The discovery of enormous natural resources in West Africa, particularly in the Gold Coast (later Ghana) and Nigeria, for industrial, nuclear and technological use gave birth to an exploitative scheme under the ECA/MSA and the Overseas Development Plan (ODP). To the public, the interest of the United States (and indeed the British) was best served by the development of economic and social stability among the masses of the people as a prelude to independence within the Commonwealth.

Nigeria was given attention during the post World War II period within the context of U.S. resolve to aid its close ally, Britain, in transiting the colonies into an independent nation within the Commonwealth. From a materialist perspective (and with respect to U.S. national security), Nigeria remained a strong source of almost three-quarters of the columbium ore imported into the United States throughout the transition era. It also remained a growing source of United States palm oil and tin particularly if Southeast Asia was to be cut off. In the final analysis, supporting British anti-Marxist policies was one of the goals pursued by the United States as part of the global denial of leftist organizations a place under the sun.

Chapter Eight
Embattled Leftists:
Late 1950s to 1965

INTRODUCTION

The nationalist governments and British officials took certain measures aimed at solidifying the future of the Anglo-Nigerian relationship. This chapter discusses these measures and Marxists' reactions to them. The background to this was the Soviet Union's new perception of Africa in 1958 (and afterwards) as well as the need for Britain to show its allies (particularly the United States of America) that London was leaving no stone unturned. The Soviet Union's new approach featured economic and technical aid to newly independent African nations by way of gaining their support in world affairs.[1]

Britain was, of course, concerned about the new Soviet interest in Africa, with all of its various solicitations of friendships. British officials were keenly interested in retaining the sympathy and support of newly independent states of Africa and preventing them from being subverted by Soviet influence.[2] It thus pursued policies aimed at sustaining the Western position in the new emerging nations in Africa, Asia, and the West Indies. While the exodus of British personnel from Nigeria on the eve of 1960 was of much concern, efforts were geared towards preserving the special relationship between ruling nationalists and colonial officials through drafting of a Technical Co-operation Scheme and a Defence Agreement, ensuring the maintenance of economic links, and promoting Nigeria's membership of the Commonwealth and its adherence to a non-neutralist foreign policy after independence. The leftist groups of course, opposed these measures because they perceived it as the prelude to underdevelopment and the continuous influence of the colonial power. Stalling the incorporation of Nigeria into the international capitalist system remained the main goal of Marxist groups during this period.[3]

In 1959, various initiatives were on the table: the Cabinet African (Official) Committee's "Future Constitutional Development in the Colonies," the Foreign Office's "Africa: The Next Ten Years," and NATO's "Report on Communist Penetration in Africa."[4] The Committee met on January 6, 1959 to consider the CO memorandum about "Future Constitutional Development in the Colonies." Agreeing that constitutional development in Nigeria had prepared it for independence within the Commonwealth, they also happily noted that, "all the governments in Nigeria have publicly condemned international communism as a threat to their own freedom."[5]

At another meeting the Committee noted that, "None of the leaders of the majority parties have sympathy with communism and none of them, except perhaps in his heart of hearts Dr. N. Azikiwe, advocates a purely 'neutralist' policy."[6] The assurance of a non-neutralist policy in world affairs and membership of the Sterling Area and the Commonwealth were to be complemented by a Technical Co-operation Scheme and a Defence Agreement. The essence of all these was to deny the USSR any advantage in post-independence Nigeria.

BACKGROUND TO NON-NEUTRALITY

In 1959, British officials were concerned about Nigeria's future role as an ally.[7] Colonial officials maintained that so long as Balewa and his peers remained at the helm of Nigerian affairs there was nothing about which to worry. They were satisfied with the outcome of the December 1959 general elections, which gave the Northern Peoples Congress (NPC) a slight majority in the parliament thereby making it a senior partner in the coalition with the National Council of Nigerian Citizens (NCNC).

Earlier in March, Northern self-government had been granted, the Eastern and Western regions having been self-governing since 1957. Balewa's success in the December 12, 1959 general elections seems to have increased the confidence of British officials.[8] They noted that Balewa had displayed remarkable wisdom and statesmanship in his capacity as a Minister, Leader of Government Business, and later as Prime Minister.[9]

The policy of non-neutralism was predicated upon Nigeria's alignment with the Western powers in world affairs. Britain could not allow Nigeria to become non-aligned in world politics because true non-alignment was precluded by its strategic location, size and potential. The Cabinet Committee concluded at one of its meetings that "Neutralist policies were not at present in favour in Nigeria; instead there was a strong pro-Commonwealth and anti-Communist feeling and it was unlikely that a substantial change in this outlook would occur, provided that the policies of the West were not such as to be completely un-acceptable to Nigerian opinion."[10]

While the British had some reservations about Azikiwe,[11] they were confident about the support and solidarity of other leading nationalists. These men included regional premiers, ministers and senior party-men who were committed to the prevention of communist infiltration.

Part of the enthusiasm for non-neutralism as part of Nigeria's post-independence foreign policy was the result of NATO's Report of 1959, which suggested that, where relevant, NATO members should ensure the support of their old colonies against the Eastern bloc.[12] It, however, added that "it would be counter-productive to attempt to prevent Soviet contacts by force; it would be better to convince the Africans that the new colonialist was the U.S.S.R. and let them experience the fact at first hand."[13] Furthermore, Britain recognized the fact that economic, commercial, cultural and emotional bonds with its old colonies were to remain intact. An editorial in *The Times* (London) summed up the situation as "a game of diplomatic *ju-jitsu,* which the contestant using the least force will win."[14]

BALEWA, THE MARXISTS AND NON-NEUTRALIST POLICY

The Prime Minister, Abubakar Tafawa Balewa, was more emphatic about non-neutrality policy on foreign affairs than any other politician was in the 1960s. He was the champion of non-neutrality in Anglophone Africa. In his reported conversation with Kwame Nkrumah in February 1959, Balewa emphatically voiced his admiration of the West and the need for non-neutrality among Africans as a way of consolidating long-term and beneficial ties with Britain (and perhaps the United States).[15] He pledged mutual support in the defense field with the United Kingdom, and was unequivocal about adoption of a neutralist line in foreign affairs.[16] As he reported, "I told him categorically that we were going to stand by the West and that we could be full partners in the British Commonwealth of Nations, that we disliked neutrality and did not believe in it."[17]

While Nigeria's membership of the Commonwealth could be seen as a *fait accompli,* the government took steps toward delaying the opening of a Russian Embassy in Nigeria.[18] The politics of delaying the opening of the USSR's Embassy in Nigeria began in January 1960, when the Foreign Office outlined strict measures that should be followed before permission would be granted to any country wishing to open an embassy in Nigeria.[19] Subsequently accreditation and opening of an embassy was based upon a Foreign

Office memorandum. This, perhaps, was responsible for the USSR's late application for opening an embassy, which was only made after October 1960 in the hope that the new regime would grant permission more easily.

They were wrong. Balewa sought the advice of the Secretary of State for Foreign and Commonwealth Affairs about the steps to be taken. As he wrote, "the Russians were being insistent about opening an embassy, and I put them off by saying that it was a question of applying in the usual way."[20] Balewa had taken the line that applications would be dealt with in the following order of priority: Commonwealth countries; countries already having offices in Lagos; and new applications according to their merits.[21]

In a conversation with Balewa, the British Secretary of State for Foreign and Commonwealth Affairs noted that the government had taken the necessary steps to stall the USSR's application.[22] This explains why the USSR had no embassy in Nigeria until 1961. The British Embassy, on the other hand, represented Nigeria in the USSR until 1962 when it opened its first mission in Moscow (the first in the Eastern bloc).

On the eve of independence, Sir James Robertson relinquished the offices of internal affairs, police, finance and economic development to Balewa and his ministers. Subsequently, the office of the Governor-General was given to Dr. Nnamdi Azikiwe. As part of the training process, Robertson had allowed Balewa to read foreign and diplomatic papers, as well as those on defense.[23] According to Robertson, this prepared Balewa for the task of handling foreign and defense matters.[24]

Adequate machinery and personnel were also set up at the External Affairs Department in Lagos and Nigeria's office at the United Nations in New York. The administrators at both offices had been trained in the United Kingdom and the United States as well as in other British Embassies. They were men for whom senior officials could vouch when it came to security and the continuity of non-neutralist policy in foreign affairs.

Beginning in 1957, Reginald Barrett, a Briton in charge of the Nigerian Liaison Office in Washington, was asked to train six mid-career Nigerians who later became Assistant Secretaries in the External Affairs Department on completion of their training. About forty in all were selected to undergo training in Washington and other British embassies. They were tutored in international relations, protocol, and diplomatic procedures, by British and U.S. officials in New York and Washington D.C. These men also offered a course on "Issues in International Relations" at the Johns Hopkins School of Advanced International Studies.[25]

One of the most important figures in the External Affairs Department during this period was L.O.V. Anionwu, who first acted as a liaison officer for Balewa's government in London. In his recommendation on July 4,

1960, the Director of the Imperial Defence College, London, Sir Robert Scott, suggested to the Foreign Office that Anionwu would be a reliable candidate for the position of a Permanent Under-Secretary of Defence and External Affairs in independent Nigeria. Anionwu had taken a series of courses on diplomacy, protocol, and international politics, and had imbibed the spirit of the international capitalist system while in the Imperial Defence College. Sir Robert Scott remarked that Anionwu was " . . . Very friendly . . . African department could, I am sure, speak to him with complete freedom about Foreign Office thinking on Nigeria . . . it would be a very good investment and well worth the trouble."[26]

It was not surprising therefore, that Anionwu became an adviser and Under-Secretary to Balewa on Defence and Foreign Affairs on the eve of independence. On the other hand, both Ifeagwu and Aig-Imoukhuede were posted to the Nigerian Permanent Mission in the United Nations in 1959 to study western diplomatic protocol. Ifeagwu had earlier served with the U.K. Consulate General in Washington for three years, before being appointed to the United Nations. Aig-Imoukhuede had worked at both the Nigerian *Daily Times* and *Sunday Times* between 1955 and 1957. Between 1957 and 1958, he was the editor of *Federal Nigeria*, a publication of the Ministry of Research and Information. His success there, as the government's image maker was perhaps responsible for his being recommended for the United Nations job by Kola Balogun, the Minister for Research and Information.

Suffice it to say then that the Nigerian Foreign Service was built upon pro-Western ideological premises. The Robertson/Balewa government was careful in its appointment and secondment of personnel to the nascent External Affairs Department. In fact, appointments or secondment into the External Affairs Department (later Ministry of External and Commonwealth Affairs) since the 1950s were based upon the ideological orientation of the individuals. This became glaring from 1957 onwards, when non-career diplomats were seconded from the civil service to the External Affairs Department.

It should not be surprising therefore, that men like Nwokedi, Simeon Adebo, N.A. Martins, Anionwu, Osakwe, Ogbu, G.M. Garba and Iyalla (all civil servants); and Mohammadu Ngileruma, Baba Gana, Abdul Maliki, J.T. Yesufu, Bello Malabu, Ignatius Durlong and Sanni Kontagora (all party stalwarts), were appointed into various positions in the Foreign Service. These were the men who executed Balewa's non-neutralist policies.

MARXISTS AND THE ANGLO-NIGERIAN DEFENSE PACT

One of the ways by which Britain satisfied its commitments to the Western bloc was the consummation and realization of a defense pact with its former colonies. In the case of Nigeria (as in other parts of the empire), the idea of a defense pact did not just emerge in 1958. If viewed from a Cold War perspective, as it should be, the idea was aimed at consolidating the gains of the Western powers generally in defense and strategy against the Soviet-led Eastern bloc. It should not be surprising therefore that the Soviet Union was the first to criticize the idea on the floor of the United Nations when it was first signed with Ceylon in 1947.

Apart from winning hearts and souls, defense strategy was also important in Anglo-American Cold War politics. Gupta and John Kent have argued that defense strategy had been part of British Cold War tactics since 1947.[27] As early as 1951, senior Colonial Office officials had identified two major roles for the colonies in defense matters. And as Trafford Smith noted, colonies played their part in defense in two ways:

(1) "By raising and maintaining forces from their local manpower. These forces have the primary role of safeguarding internal security in their territories, thereby preserving the usefulness of the territories as bases and sources of manpower, raw materials, etc; and,

(2) By maintaining or increasing their contribution to the pool of economic resources available for the Commonwealth war effort."[28]

This view suggests, then, that the thrust of the Anglo-Nigerian defense pact was the need to sustain Britain's influence in Nigeria after independence.

As spelled out in the policy paper, "Defence Policy and Global Strategy" in March 1952, Britain's obligation was based on its role in Europe, NATO, and the Commonwealth, as well as London's desire to remain a leading power. Africa was not left out of the overall defense strategy. Lord Salisbury noted in July 1954 that, "Britain was to continue to play an eminent role in checking the spread of communism; she was to preserve security and develop stable government in colonial territories."[29]

Two short-term steps were taken towards realizing this. First was the encouragement of defense co-operation conferences with other colonial powers, South Africa and the United States. Two conferences were held in Nairobi and Dakar in August 1951 and March 1954 respectively. Second, based upon the Ministry of Defence Official Committee's recommendation on August 15, 1955, the Cabinet approved the appointment of a military adviser in East and West Africa, if administering officers and local politicians finally approved of it.[30]

As to long-term measures, Sir Harold Parker (Permanent Secretary— Ministry of Defence, 1948–1956) noted that "We should hope that the West African territories on achieving independence would agree to undertake some external defence commitment, on the lines of the present commitment to provide a Brigade for use in a major war, as part of the obligations arising from Commonwealth membership."[31]

Officials in the colonies were directed to seek the views of local politicians as soon as the opportunity arose. In Nigeria, Britain used the opportunity of the constitutional conferences in late 1957 and 1958 to seek the views of politicians as to the desirability of a defense pact after independence. Contrary to general opinion, Nigerians were not coerced into signing the Defence Pact with the United Kingdom in 1960.[32] First, the final decision about the pact rested upon Parliament's approval and the signature of the Prime Minister after independence. This procedure was adopted after the USSR's criticism of a similar pact with Ceylon earlier in 1947.[33] Secondly, available evidence suggests that Nigerian politicians viewed it as part of the good will and cooperation between the two countries. In fact, Nigerian politicians believed that it would ensure the territorial integrity of the nascent nation and help defend her from external aggression.[34]

Towards the end of 1958, the Prime Minister, Federal Ministers and the three Regional Premiers agreed to enter into a defense agreement with Britain after independence. Azikiwe had earlier taken the view that it would be in the interests of Nigeria and Great Britain to sign a defense agreement whereby the UK would have "full facilities to use Kano and Lagos airfields for the transport of troops and supplies in peace or war time; to use the harbors of Lagos and Port Harcourt and the communications thence with Kano."[35] Amongst the reasons for these was that any loss of airfield facilities at Kano would have a serious effect on Britain's ability to safeguard her interests in the Indian Ocean in the post-independence period.[36] In addition Nigeria could not at the time afford the huge cost of training her military personnel and the buying of military equipment.

The United Kingdom's Defence Pact with Nigeria, like those with Ceylon, Malaya and the Gold Coast, should be seen as part of a general desire to sustain Western interests in peace and war. It was, in part, a political move to prevent the subversive influence of the USSR. As the Foreign Office noted: "We have certain requirements in Africa which need to be examined . . . they partly derived from considerations of internal security and partly from considerations of global strategic policy."[37]

This involved the presence in Kenya of element of Britain's strategic reserves; aircraft staging rights in Nigeria, Gambia, Sierra Leone and Kenya; and rights to over-fly territories between the staging points. In return for the use of Nigerian airfields, harbors and ports, Britain agreed to train Nigerian army and naval personnel in the United Kingdom.[38] While a significant proportion of the cost was to be paid by Nigeria, Her Majesty's Government nonetheless assisted in defraying part of it. The Nigerian Parliament passed the bill by a vote of 149 to 39 on November 19, 1960.[39] Official signing of the treaty between the two governments did not take place until January 5, 1961.

Nigerian youth were, however, not happy with the defense pact. It presented Marxists with an opportunity to revive their idea that the whole process of decolonization and the transfer of power were aimed at creating a neo-colonial dependency and a fertile international capitalist system in the country.[40] As Claude Phillips noted: "From the beginning of independence, Nigeria has faced a bewildering array of internal pressures attempting to establish, alter, or repudiate the foreign policy of the country." He concluded, "the articulate challenges against the government were by no means limited to parliament." According to him, "Non-governmental groups such as political parties, labor unions, university student unions, youth groups, newspapers, and others joined the radical politicians in condemning Government actions and policies."[41]

Under the leadership of a Soviet trained pharmacist, Tunji Otegbeye, the Nigerian Youth Congress, the Zikist National Vanguard, and the National University Students' Union staged several protests in Lagos and other parts of the country.[42] They identified five obnoxious aspects of the pact. These were

- "If a British soldier kills a Nigerian he cannot be tried in the courts of Nigeria, but can be acquitted on the strength of a mere exonerating statement by a British superior;
- The British soldiers have an unlimited right to carry guns wherever they go in Nigeria. Yet no Nigerian can carry arms without permission from the Governor-General;
- Nigeria guarantees to the British soldiers full exemption from passport and visa formalities;
- The British soldiers are entitled to complete fiscal immunities, full exemption from exchange regulations, and absolute freedom from customs duties and inspection at ports of entry; and,
- All vehicles of the British servicemen are exempted from all licensing and insurance regulations."[43]

Because of the many serious disturbances that followed, Balewa's government had no option other than to abrogate the defense pact in January 1962. Nigerian military personnel, however, continued to receive training in the United Kingdom despite the abrogation.

MARXISTS AND OTHER IMPERIAL PREFERENCES

Linking the economy with the Sterling Area[44] and Nigerian membership in the Commonwealth were significant parts of the anti-leftist decolonizing policies pursued by British officials and the Balewa government before independence. The colonial economy, unsurprisingly, was closely linked with Britain and the Sterling Area. It was principally based on the production and export of primary produce, the price of which depended on world trade. There was an increase in the volume of exports of primary produce from Nigeria to Western countries, particularly Britain, during the period. Whether or not this led to development or under-development is another debate.[45] What is of interest here is that the economy was linked with the Sterling Area as part of the efforts towards cementing a financial relationship between Britain and her colonies.[46]

In official circles, preference for the Sterling Area was linked with the future of the Commonwealth.[47] As early as 1953, Sir Norman Brook, Secretary to the Cabinet (1947–1962), wrote a memorandum, which later became a Cabinet paper: "The Future of Commonwealth Membership." Brook argued that, Britain should aim to keep colonies, which could expect independence in the next ten or twenty years, solidly in the Commonwealth after independence. His argument was that through this Britain would maintain the political cohesion of the Sterling Area.[48] This idea was supported by most senior colonial officials, particularly Sir Hilton Poynton (Deputy Under-Secretary of State, 1948-August 1959). He stressed that Britain should strengthen moves towards the political cohesion of the Sterling Area and the Commonwealth.[49] He raised three questions and provided answers to them. These were (1) "Will the territories in category [a] be willing to remain in the Sterling Area when independent? (2) Could their continued membership of the Sterling Area be made a condition of their membership of the Commonwealth? and (3) Would their continued membership of the Sterling Area, whether within or without the Commonwealth, be a source of strength?"[50]

As to question one, Poynton noted that much depended upon the success of the Sterling Area in international trade. "Decisions," according to Poynton, "will be taken on their own judgment of self-interest, though one naturally hopes that judgment will lead them to remain within the Sterling Area."[51] In his answer to the second question he argued that, "we could not make continued membership of the Sterling Area a condition of full membership of the Commonwealth, partly because Canada is already outside the Sterling Area but inside the Commonwealth."[52] He concluded "the crucial point is really not membership of the Commonwealth but membership of the Sterling Area."[53]

This was, perhaps, why the Cabinet Africa Official Committee in its meeting in January 1959 concluded that: "The Sterling area would suffer a moderate loss of dollar exchange if Nigeria were to leave it; departure from the Commonwealth, without leaving the Sterling area, would have little or no effect on the latter."[54] Officials, however, were confident that Nigeria would remain in the Commonwealth after independence. Their assurance was based on Nigerian politicians' preference for membership of the Commonwealth, which they believed would strengthen their relationship with the United Kingdom.[55] Much, however, depended upon whether or not ex-masters and ex-servants remained always as friends.

A key factor in the future relationship between Nigeria and the United Kingdom was the extent of the latter's economic aid for development after independence.[56] In 1959 for instance, the Foreign Office stated that Russia's tactics in Africa had changed considerably. There was now more Soviet economic aid to newly independent African states, such as Guinea, Ghana and Egypt. As the FO memorandum stated, "their technique is at present to represent themselves as an alternative source of economic and technical help."[57]

The Cabinet Africa (Official) Committee deliberated upon the FO's memorandum on January 21, 1959. As it relates to Nigeria, members concluded that "It would be of the highest value if, in agreement with Nigerian leaders, arrangements could be made before independence for the introduction at that time of a technical co-operation scheme similar in form, but larger in size, than that which had been introduced for Ghana."[58] The Committee suggested that the CO should circulate a memorandum discussing the means of encouraging economic development in Nigeria, with a view to the possible formulation of a technical co-operation scheme.[59]

The Cabinet Africa (Official) Committee met on February 20, 1959, to discuss the CO memorandum on technical co-operation scheme for Nigeria. At the meeting, C.G. Eastwood (Assistant Under-Secretary of State, 1955–1965) presented the CO memorandum that set out the possible lines on which a scheme of technical co-operation with post-independence Nigeria might be developed.[60] The memorandum proposed a bilateral scheme (which was heavily weighted towards UK assistance at the outset) rather than an international or Commonwealth multilateral plan.[61]

The Colonial Office was of the view that "the scheme would need to be on a generous scale so that our effort compared reasonably favourably with those of other countries . . ."[62] The Cabinet Committee concluded that the United Kingdom was bound to make a contribution to Nigerian development, and that the need for a technical assistance scheme should be acceptable in principle.[63] The Treasury was, however, asked to determine how much could be used in this way.[64] Like the Defence Agreement, Nigerian leaders accepted the offer of a Technical Co-operation Scheme after independence. This was the genesis of Nigeria/UK bilateral co-operation in education, agriculture, science and technology after independence.

By late 1959 one can arguably say that Britain, with the assistance of leading politicians, had shaped the world outlook of most Nigerians towards the West. No doubt the ideological orientation of the Nigerian ruling elite was pro-Western: the principle of "free enterprise" and "perpetuation of capitalist economy" were dominant perceptions in Nigerian economic and developmental program. A "nurtured-capitalism" had been established. What remained was its consolidation after independence.[65] Upon successful completion of the general elections of December 1959, the Secretary of State for the Colonies introduced the Nigerian Independence Bill to the House of Commons that was unanimously passed. At this point in late 1959 and early 1960, the British could not afford to risk what they had striven hard to build—the confidence and respect of Nigerian politicians—by refusing or delaying independence. On October 1, 1960, power was eventually transferred to Nigerian politicians with the hope that Britain and Nigeria would remain as allies.

MARXISTS AND THE NEW NATION

In late 1960 a group of returning Soviet-trained Nigerians and ex-Zikists formed the Nigerian Youth Congress. The Congress, as could be expected, was guided by Marxist ideology and did not hide its admiration for Soviets' reorientation of its African policy. The change from a Stalinist view of Marxist-Leninist transition in Africa to Premier Khrushchev's understanding of the nationalist stage as a natural stage in the transition to a socialist revolution was important in the overall success of the Marxist vanguards in Nigeria. The NYC and its allied Zikist National Vanguard were opposed to Anglo-American influence in Nigeria and the pro-Western foreign policy of the Balewa administration. The domestic policy of the government was also criticized from time to time as being tailored to benefit the rich rather than the masses.

The Marxists, however, made some progress through article publications in pro-Western newspapers and the various government controlled press and communication media. It was through the press that the Marxists were able to call on Balewa's government to stop the witch-hunting of Marxists and other radical groups. It was not surprising therefore that the Marxists implored the government to change its domestic policy of non-employment of Eastern-bloc trained Nigerians in the public sector. The government was also asked to lift the ban on the importation of Communist literature because it was a negation of the right of the Nigerian citizens to get information on any subject or topic of interest.[66]

Members of the NYC and ZNV were also opposed to Western interference in independent African nations' domestic situation as in the Lumumba case. In February 15, 1961, the Marxists under the leadership of a Soviet-trained medical practitioner, Tunji Otegbeye, organized a riot in response to the assassination of Patrice Lumumba and the Anglo-Nigerian defense pact.[67] Although the government quickly quelled the riot and arrested its organizers, Marxist groups seem to have made progress in making themselves relevant in the new nation's politics.[68]

It seems that the Balewa government was conscious of the situation and the trend in Marxian organisation. The government responded by convening the All-Nigeria People's Conference in August 1961. The idea, it seems, was not "merely a means of allowing the radicals to let off steam," as Phillips would have us believe.[69] It was a genuine response on the part of the government to address sensitive issues that affected the new nation. The opportunity created was historic, because for the first time leftist groups were able to air their views without intimidation and repression.

The leftists regarding Nigeria's foreign policy made a lot of noise. The International Relations Committee under Aminu Kano concluded that government policy was pro-West and anti-Soviet. It made four recommendations as follow:

(a) "The government should desist from communist witch-hunting";
(b) "The Soviet should be given accommodations equal to that any nation";
(c) "The Soviet Union should have equal facilities as other diplomatic missions";
(d) "Mr. Khrushchev should be invited to visit Nigeria."[70]

These views were not surprising to the government because it had been one of the publicly debated issues between the government and the leftist groups. Possibly, one of the effects of these recommendations was that the government allowed the opening of a Soviet Union Embassy in Lagos, although with some restrictions.

In late 1961, Chukwudolue Orhakamalu and Obong Udoeka announced the formation of a Communist Party of Nigeria in Kano. The choice of "holy" Kano is surprising because leftist groups had always operated in the southern part of Nigeria. The group was not seen as a threat, and the government's attitude was to downplay its existence. In fact, between late 1961 and early 1964, the group made no significant impact on politics and development in Nigeria. But the Federal election of 1964 soon changed its silent attitude. An advertisement was placed in the *West African Pilot* sponsored by the Communist Party of Nigeria calling for an "Operation Mobilisation."[71]

"Operation Mobilisation" was an attempt by CPN leadership to recruit members among the populace and, more importantly, to enjoin them to participate during the forthcoming elections. To Chukwudolue Orhakamalu (president) and Obong Udoeka Esiet (general secretary), the goal was to beat the right-wing politicians in popularity and draw more sympathy from the population. Mobilizing the masses was seen as the first effort to attaining power. The CPN also hoped to field candidates and contest for various positions during the election of 1964. As events showed, the efforts were unsuccessful.

Instead, another leftist organisation under the leadership of Dr. Tunji Otegbeye contested the election of 1964 using the name Socialist Workers and Farmers Party of Nigeria (SWFPN). Formed in 1963, it registered as a political party in 1964 to contest the upcoming Federal elections. The SWFPN was more successful than any previous attempts at nationwide leftist organizations in Nigeria. The strategy was to affiliate with the Nigerian Trade Union Congress (NTUC), which was sponsored by the Moscow-funded World Federation of Trade Unions (WFTU). Through NTUC, funds were sent to SWFPN to carry out its activities in Nigeria.[72]

Both Otegbeye and Wahab Goodluck enjoyed the confidence of the Soviet Union and Communist International between 1963 and 1966. The idea of scientific socialism was the basis of SWFPN campaign during the elections of 1964. The Soviet Union donated a sum of £75,000 towards SWFPN campaign and other activities during this period. While the party did not succeed in making any impact on the electorate because of its poor performance during the elections, it did have an impact in other areas. Working closely with the NTUC, SWFPN used fund from the Soviet Union to establish Eko Printers and the Socialist Publishing House. Through these institutions, a newspaper called *"Advance"* was published with the aim of disseminating the ideas of scientific socialism in Nigeria.

Otegbeye seems to have benefited more because the Soviet fund was used to set up Ireti Clinic and Tutu "Kemists." Thus, he was able to practice medicine since he could not find employment in government hospitals. The clinic and pharmacy were seen as a leftist gesture to Otegbeye and his cohorts for their efforts. As it could be expected, the beneficiaries of leftist organizations' goodwill (such as scholarships or donations) were kin and kindred of SWAFP leadership. Dedicated members of the NTUC and SWFPN also benefited by being appointed into office to compensate for their efforts. Wahab Goodluck, Kunle Oyero, and Eskor Toyo were appointed as directors of the West African Engineering and Automobile Company (WAATECO) and the Patrice Lumumba Academy of Labour and Political Science respectively.[73]

While preventing Marxists from participating in the administration of Nigeria during the 1960s, the government was challenged and criticized for not getting aid from non-capitalist nations in order to meet the requirements of the First National Development Plan (1962–1968). In 1961, two key federal ministers, Zana Dipcharima (Commerce and Industry) and Waziri Ibrahim (Health, and later Economic Development) remarked that it was stupendous and foolish not to seek aid from the Soviet bloc in view of the inability of the West to satisfy Nigeria's aid and assistance for the first six-year plan. By 1964, the Western region Governor, Odeleye Fadahunsi, not only received Soviet Union's delegation, but remarked that "any assistance that the a Soviet Union could render towards the implementation of Nigeria's Six-Year development Plan would be appreciated by the Federal Government."[74]

Dipcharima and Waziri's comments no doubt influenced the inclusion of Moscow on the itinerary of the first Nigerian economic mission to Europe in May 1961. The goal was to seek economic and technical assistance favorable to Nigeria. As it relates to the Soviet Union, this meant economic and developmental goal were distinguished from the implications of ideology or Cold War politics. Moreover, the Nigerian leadership was interested in opening up technological cooperation without ideological indoctrination during the visit. Although not much was achieved during the 1961 visit led by Festus Okotie-Eboh (Finance Minister), the government continued its pragmatic approach towards the Soviet Union.

Much was, however, achieved between 1962 and early 1966, when it seems that the Nigerian government had removed some barriers to relations with the Soviet Union. In August 1962 for instance, Dipcharima told newspaper reporters that, the "Federal Government had been progressively dismantling whatever barriers that existed in the flow of trade between Nigeria and the Communist bloc."[75] This statement was perhaps influential in the Eastern bloc participation during the Lagos International Trade Fair in September of 1962. The Soviet bloc was not only given a good reception by the president, Nnamdi Azikiwe, the fair boosted trade with Nigeria thereafter. By June 1963, both Nigeria and the Soviet Union had signed a bilateral agreement for trade and exchange in cocoa, timber, tin and columbite, rubber, textiles, cement, chemical products and automobiles. Although the percentage of trade with the Soviet bloc remained low, the continuous interest and visitation from both sides increased between 1963 and 1966.

CONCLUSION

In conclusion, this chapter has highlighted the transition between the colonial power and the Nigerian intelligentsia that assumed power in 1960, with particular attention to the continuity of anti-leftist policies and the transformation of Nigeria into the capitalist system. Leftist groups were unsuccessful in efforts to gain control of the political economy after independence largely because British policies had well equipped the indigenous ruling elite with anti-leftist tactics. While pragmatism was the key to dealing with external leftist influences from the Soviet bloc, a "McCarthyian" strategy was adopted against leftists "within." As the next chapter will show, this explains the success of the ruling pro-West nationalist and labor leaders and the failure of leftist groups in Nigeria.

Chapter Nine

Conclusion: Assessing Marxism Failure

INTRODUCTION

Throughout the decolonization period, leading nationalists and Anglo-American officials were certain that, at least, imperative—Marxism must be thwarted as a nationwide ideology in Nigeria. Anglo-American officials frequently warned leading nationalists about the danger and horrors of leftist ideology and gave them all necessary tools to combat its survival. They were not only convinced that leftist ideology was not in the best interest of Nigeria but were worried about the use of violence and bloodshed to attain and maintain such power.

This chapter focuses on plausible reasons for the failure of leftist ideology and organizations in Nigeria. In contrast to the West Indies and Malaya, where Britain engaged in military action to suppress leftist ideology,[1] efforts in Nigeria were non-combative. British efforts were geared towards administrative reforms, improved security and intelligence, political appointments and rewards, constitutional change, summer school training, counter-propaganda and collaboration.[2]

CONTEMPORARY ASSESSMENTS OF MARXISM'S FAILURE IN NIGERIA

Among the earliest assessments of the Marxist failure in Nigeria were reports from the Communist Party of Great Britain's (CPGB) fact-finding missions to Nigeria in 1951. For instance, Idise Dafe's (formerly of Eze's *Labour Champion*) "Report on visit to Nigeria" is an acknowledgment of the failure of the Marxists in Nigeria.[3] As part of an effort to see whether Communism has gained some ground in Nigeria, Idise Dafe was sent in

1951 to tour the country and assess efforts being made by CPGB members that had returned to Nigeria since the late 1940s and the early 1950s. Dafe, it should be noted was a recipient of Eze's *Labour Champion* and the *Daily Worker* (London) training arrangement, who joined the CPGB upon arrival in England early in 1950.

Dafe's "Report" was not only pessimistic, but a testimony as to the ineffectiveness and episodic nature of the several Marxist groups in Nigeria during the period. He identified various causes, including a leadership crisis, incoherence and rigid government measures as reasons for the failure of Communism in Nigeria.[4] He lamented that "Our Nigerian comrades do return to our fatherland and that is all we hear of them."[5]

In 1956, Palme Dutt also admitted the failure of communism in Nigeria despite various attempts since the late 1940s to form a united communist front. He added as a factor for its failure the fact that "there was considerable disagreement in estimating the political forces . . . and any differences of estimation in our press and other organs of the international Communist movement are quickly taken advantage of by the enemies of Communism in Nigeria."[6]

Samuel Ikoku has identified two main reasons for the failure of Marxist groups in Nigeria. First is the embedded internal crisis with the groups. And second is the sustained "right-wing" offensive in the trade union movement. The uncooperative nature of such anti-imperialist trade unions such as Mba's Government Catering Workers Union, Egwnwoke's Marine Engine Room and Deck Ratings African Workers Union, Obasa's Postal and Telegraph Linemen Union, Awobiyi's Seamen's Union, Ejit Agwu's Elder Dempter Workers Union, Nwasiashi's Union of Native Administrative Servants, Nwana's Locomotive Drivers Union, etc, prevented a coordinated orientation of the unions into mainstream leftist group.

Perhaps of much serious consequence is the sustained "right-wing" offensive against Marxist leaders and followers. As Ikoku perceptively states "the greatest blow to our activities has been the total collapse of the Eze faction both in the N.L.C. and in the U.A.C. African Workers Union." He continued his lamentation by stating that, "our plans largely involved using this group (Eze group) of trade unionists as a lever for re-organising the movement."[7]

NIGERIAN RELIGIONS VERSUS ATHEIST MARXISM

Another explanation for the failure of leftist ideology lies in the religious beliefs of the people. By late 1930s, the dominant religions in Nigeria were Christianity, Islam and traditional religions. While Islam permeated the

Northern Region, large numbers of Muslims could also be found in the south, particularly in the Western Region during the same period. Christianity was also important in the south. One remarkable aspect of both religions is that they are both foreign (non-indigenous) to the peoples of present day Nigeria. Within a single family, even in the North, one could find a Muslim, a Christian, and a practitioner of traditional religion. The belief in the existence of God is common to all religion.[8]

The Marxian idea that religion is the opiate of the masses had a stronghold on many communists. This is partly why most nationalists, particularly the northern leaders, as inherently contrary to their own beliefs and aspirations, viewed communism. As a U.S. official noted in February 1953, "Northern political leaders are in complete opposition to the antigovernment activities or communism taking place in the south of Nigeria."[9]

For instance, Sir Ahmadu Bello, the Sardauna of Sokoto, and the first premier of Northern Region, saw himself not only as a political leader but also as the spiritual leader of the North, whose duty it was to spread Islam to all parts of the country.[10] Similarly, Nnamdi Azikiwe and Michael Okpara, the Eastern Region leaders, and Obafemi Awolowo and Samuel Akintola, the Western Region Leaders, did not hide their dislike of Marxism.[11] Since Marxism was opposed to religion, it was bound to fail in Nigeria, either during the colonial or the post-colonial era, as many people were religious. Melady was therefore correct in his conclusion that "the Nigerian people, firm in religious traditions, whether Muslim or Christian, do not offer a fertile market for the communists."[12]

Earlier evidence of antagonism towards leftist ideology in Nigeria is to be found in Reverend Father A. Foley's lecture titled, "Catholic and Communism" published in the *Daily Comet* of October 30, 1948. Comparing press freedom in the Soviet Union and Nigeria, he noted that Nigeria officials were more liberal.[13] He noted that freedom of speech and the press was a sham in Russia, where "one is not free to select a job for him or establish a profitable business."[14] This view is supported by a nationalist, labor and Muslim leader, H.P. Adebola, when he stated that "I, personally, as a Muslim detest what Communist Russia has been doing to the Muslims in Asia."[15]

Furthermore, Foley told his readers that the leftist ideology had no room for religion and morality. He advised all Catholics and Christians generally to dread it. He admonished his readers to " . . . Insure that the helping hand so warmly stretched forth does not slip unnoticed to their throats and stifle in their infancy hard won freedoms of democracy or perhaps extinguish for generations legitimate aspirations for independence, nationalism and self-determination."[16] To Reverend Foley and his peers, independence thus became legitimate only if nationalists and labor unionists were prepared to prevent the formation of a leftist organisation in Nigeria. The editorials of *The Nigerian Catholic Herald,* a weekly publication of the St. Paul Catholic Press of Ebute-Metta, Lagos, and an organ of Nigeria's National Catholic Church, supported this view.[17]

As late as 1961, the U.S. based Christian Anticommunist Crusade (CACC) was in support of Nigerian Christian Leaders' Conference (NCLC) and the Nigeria based Pocket Testament League's (PTL) anti-leftism in postcolonial Nigeria. Formed in early 1953 at Waterloo, Iowa by Drs. W.E. Pietsch and Fred Schwarz, education, evangelism, and dedication remained the core program of CACC anticommunism worldwide. As Schwarz noted "our basic thesis is that Communism must be studied in depth." He continued by stating "We therefore endeavor to study and expound the philosophy, strategy, morality, organization and local tactics of Communism as the foundation for an enlightened anti-Communist program." This, he considered to be "a responsible approach."[18]

While we cannot at the moment identify total number of members in Don McFarlene's led Pocket Testament League and the Nigerian Christian Leaders' Conference, we can infer that membership was larger than identified Marxists during the period. In response to PTL request the CACC sent educational materials to counter Marxists momentum of early 1960 through 1962. Thus, a large supply of literature for NCLC was sent through PTL in 1961 costing the organization a total sum of $6,000. These included *"You Can Trust the Communists," "The Christian Answer to Communism," "The Heart, Mind and Soul of Communism," "The Communist Interpretation of Peace," "Communism-Diagnosis and Treatment," "Communism—A Disease," and "Communism—A Religion."* While we cannot gauge the amount of success these books had on the populace, we can state that it was a useful tool of education for Christians and anti-Communists generally.[19]

THE ROLE OF THE PRESS

Another explanation for the failure of Marxism is the role of the leading newspapers and their editorial comments. Despite various press reports of Cominform interest in Nigeria, which were often reprinted by Eze's *Labour Champion* (established in February 1950) and Ikoku's *Nigerian Socialist Review* (established in 1952), the press generally was not in favor of Marxism as an alternative to British colonialism. Moreover both the *Labour Champion* and the *Nigerian Socialist Review* enjoyed a few readers limited to Marxists in the south.

Most leading and widely circulated newspapers were pro-government and anti-leftist in their editorials. In fact the Zikist Movement leadership was shocked to the core when the *West African Pilot,* hitherto known for its anti-British sentiments, began to attack Marxists in an editorial, which rasped that, "no greater treachery can be inflicted by anybody upon the cause of Nigerian freedom than to import communism into this country."[20] The editorial further described the leftists as "a clique of muddled brained individuals who talk glibly on the principal ideology of which they have not even the foggiest idea."[21]

Some of the newspapers also published negative reports about leftist states in Europe in order to dissuade Nigerians from imbibing leftist ideas. An example was an editorial published by J. V. Clinton in the *Nigerian Eastern Mail.* Willard Quincy Stanton, the United States Consul General in Lagos reported that the "paper has a circulation of about 2,500 and is frequently moderate in tone as well as friendly to American interests."[22] Clinton was not, however, totally in support of the West. Writing in an editorial of November 25, 1950, he told his readers not to be a partisan in the Cold War between the Eastern and Western blocs.[23] As he noted, "as a West African nationalist, and even one who dislikes communism, we cannot be wholehearted partisan in the quarrel between the Communist World and the Western capitalist World."[24] This, to him, was the only righteous path to self-government and independence in Nigeria, and indeed, other parts of British West Africa.

In fact, CPGB research about main newspapers and their political/ideological interests in Nigeria during the period show that there were more newspapers in support of government than the Marxists. As at May 1952, thirteen of these were identified. These were

(1) "West African Pilot—Reformist and bourgeois nationalism, owned by Zik."
(2) "Nigerian Tribune—Conservative bourgeois intellectualism."
(3) "The People—Conservative bourgeois businessmen."
(4) "Daily Service—Conservative bourgeois intellectualism."
(5) "Eastern States Express—Conservative bourgeois intellectualism."
(6) "Eastern Guardian, Southern Defender and Nigerian Spokesman— controlled by West African Pilot."
(7 "Peoples Voice—Bourgeois reformism."
(8) "Daily Success—bourgeois nationalism. Owned by a limited liability trading company."
(9) "The Citizen and 22 weeklies and periodicals—imperialist and owned by the Gaskiya Corporation (a newspaper corporation

maintained by funds supplied by the Nigerian Government and the Colonial Development Fund)."

(10) "Daily Times—imperialist and owned by the London Daily Mirror."

(11) "Nigerian Review—imperialist and owned by the Public Relations Department of the Nigerian Government."[25]

POLITICAL LEADERS AND PRO-BRITISH LEANINGS

The choice of a post-colonial leader for Nigeria was also instrumental in the failure of leftist ideology. After the December 1959 elections and the success of NPC/NCNC coalition, this was not difficult.[26] Sir James Robertson, the Governor-General on the eve of the transfer of power, came straight to the point when he wrote that, "When a Prime Minister had to be appointed in 1959, the choice was not difficult. Balewa was the choice."[27]

Three reasons are plausible. Firstly, Balewa was pro-British to the core; secondly, he was more accommodating than Ahmadu Bello; and thirdly he believed in the north first, then Nigeria.[28] The third reason is however questionable as Clark's biography of Tafawa Balewa shows. Balewa was interested above all in the unity of Nigeria. In fact, his party declared as one of its aims the preservation of regional autonomy of the north within a united Nigeria.[29] He did not hide his dislike for Marxism and was at the forefront of its failure in Nigeria. Indeed, he was the "Nigerian-McCarthy" of the period.

The failure of leftist ideology in Nigeria was also due to the Marxists' inability to actualize their goal of revolutionary take-over from 1948 on (the year they called for a positive action against all forms of British colonial policy in Nigeria). They were also unable to penetrate the minds of a greater number of the people. Their organization could not match the rapidity with which the colonial administration responded to a "Call for Revolution." They noted in their memoirs that they lacked the mass support to actualize their dream—revolution.[30]

The inability to enlist or recruit popular support at the grassroots level accounts for the organizational failure of Marxism during the period. The division between Eze and Ikoku group discussed in ChapterThree is one factor. Perhaps of much relevance was the insignificant number of landless peasantry and proletariats in Nigeria. While these accounts for the failure of leftist ideology, we must stress that immersion and permeation of the thought among the few educated Leftists, was at best the highest level of Marxists' success.

In fact, former members of the CPGB upon returning to Nigeria had to abandon the "revolution" as well. This, perhaps, might have been influenced by Government's desire to deal with known communists or their sympathizers. These groups might have realized that colonial administration had succeeded in its various anti-leftist measures prior to their arrival. For instance, Bankole Akpata warned "fellow travelers," who had returned to West Africa before him, not to engage in "a romantic revolution." Marika Sherwood notes that in one of his letters to Nkrumah in 1948, Akpata warned that " . . . mass enthusiasm can never be a substitute for a strong and disciplined mass organization."[31] Nwabufo Uweicha, another former CPGB member, noted that the revolution had to be postponed until after independence because to engage in a revolution would prolong independence in the colonies.[32] Nevertheless, the leftists did not make much impact after independence due to continuous anti-leftist policies by the regional and central governments.

In brief, Britain also enjoyed the support of Bello, Balewa, Azikiwe and Awolowo, undoubtedly the personalities around whom devolution revolved during the period. Some leading labor leaders, such as, Adio-Moses, Esua, Porbeni, Egwuwonike, Adebola, Borha, Cole, etc; also contributed to the failure of leftist ideology in Nigeria. Also organizations such as the British TUC, ICFTU, MRM, the British Council, etc played an important role in the process. It was with the support of these men and organizations that the Colonial State was able to effectively controlled leftist ideology from penetrating into Nigeria. Both the colonial state and post-independent governments instituted a system that prevented leftist organizations from partaking in the governance of Nigeria in a post-independence period.[33]

CONCLUSION

In the final analysis, anti-leftist policies in Nigeria not only kept pace with the decolonization process, it partly created a class of political leaders who, at independence, willingly continued the tradition. The idea was to isolate the extremists and help consolidate the position of the moderate Nigerian politicians. This implied in official circles the simultaneous cultivation of individual liberal nationalist leaders and the repression of the Marxists. These were followed by constitutional reforms, development planning and anti-leftist measures. Once this was successful, Britain willingly transferred power in Nigeria. The successful implementation of various anti-leftist policies since 1945 and support from leading nationalists largely explain the failure of Marxism in Nigeria.

Notes

NOTES TO CHAPTER ONE

1. In this category are: AZ Rubinstein, *Communist Political Systems* (New Jersey, 1966); DW Treadgold, (ed.) *Soviet and Chinese Communism* (Seattle, 1973); GK Bertsch, & TW Ganschow, *Comparative Communism: The Soviet, Chinese, and Yugoslav Models* (San Francisco, 1976); RG Wesson, *Communism and Communist Systems* (New Jersey, 1978); MA Kaplan, (ed.) *The Many Faces of Communism* (New York, 1978); A Westoby, *The Evolution of Communism* (Oxford, 1989); RJC Young, *Postcolonialism: An Historical Introduction* (Massachusetts/Oxford, 2001).

2. JS Coleman, *Nigeria: Background to Nationalism* (Berkeley, 1958); GO Olusanya, *The Second World War and Politics in Nigeria, 1939–1953* (London, 1973); R Sklar, *Nigerian Political Parties: Power in an Emergent African Nation* (Princeton, 1963). Despite Sklar's analyses of party ideologies, he like Coleman did not relate them to anti-Communist policy and decolonization. See pp 265-276.

3. A Ajala, *Pan-Africanism: Evolution, Progress and Prospects* (London, 1973); PO Esedebe, *Pan-Africanism: The Idea and Movement, 1776–1963* (London, 1982); JA Langley, *Pan-Africanism and Nationalism in West Africa, 1900–1945: A Study in Ideology and Social Class* (Oxford, 1973); C Legum, *Pan-Africanism: A Short Political Guide* (London, 1965); K Nkrumah, *Revolutionary Path* (London, 1964); *Handbook of Revolutionary Warfare: A Guide to the Armed Phase of the Africa Revolution* (London, 1968); *Consciencism: Philosophy and Ideology for Decolonization* (New York, 1964); G Padmore, *Communism or Pan-Africanism? The Coming Struggle for Africa* (London, 1956); SG Ikoku, *Nigeria for Nigerians: A Study of Contemporary Nigerian Politics from a Socialist Point of View* (Takoradi, 1962); OS Osoba, "The Development of Trade Unionism in Colonial and Post-Colonial Nigeria," in IA Akinjogbin, & OS Osoba, (eds.) *Topics on Nigerian Economic and Social History* (Ile-Ife, 1980); "The Transition to Neo-colonialism," in T Falola, (ed.) *Britain and Nigeria: Development or Underdevelopment?* (New Jersey, 1987); "Ideological

Trends in the Nigerian National Liberation Movement and the Problems of National Identity, Solidarity and Motivation, 1935–1965: A Preliminary Assessment" *Ibadan,* October 1969, p 35; P Waterman, "Communist Theory in the Nigerian Trade Union Movement," in *Politics and Society,* 3,3, 1973; E Madunagu, *The Tragedy of the Nigerian Socialist Movement* (Calabar, 1980), p 2; CA Alade, "From a Bourgeois to Social Democrat: A Study in the evolution of Awolowo's concept of Ideology," in Oyelaran *et al op.cit:* p 315; Zachernuk, P. "Awolowo's Economic Thought in Historical Perspectives," in Oyelaran *op.cit.* p 283; Both Alade and Zachernuk agree that Awolowo, like his contemporaries, was "a pro-West, arch-capitalist and anti-Communist" during the colonial period. Zachernuk, P. *Colonial Subjects: An African Intelligentsia and Atlantic Ideas* (Virginia, 2000).

4. S Narasingha, "Nigerian Intellectuals and Socialism: Retrospect and Prospect," *Journal Modern African Studies, 31, 3,* 1993, pp 361-385.

5. LP Frank, "Ideological Competition in Nigeria: Urban Populism versus Elite Nationalism," *Journal of Modern African Studies, 17, 3,* September 1979, pp 433–452.

6. AO Lawal, "Britain and the Decolonisation of Nigeria, 1945–1960," PhD History Thesis, University of Ibadan, Nigeria, 1991. Siyan Oyeweso, *Mokwugo Okoye: Struggle for National Liberation and Social Justice* (Lagos: Multivision, 2003).

7. N Eze, *"Memoirs of a Crusader,"* n.d.; U Uyilawa, *The Rise and Fall of the Zikist Movement, 1946-1950* (Lagos, 1983); T Abdul Raheem & A Olukoshi, "The Left in Nigerian Politics and Struggle for Socialism, 1945-1986," in *Review of African Political Economy, No.37,* 1986; T Falola, & AG Adebayo, "The Context: The Political Economy of Colonial Nigeria" in OO Oyelaran, et al (eds.) *Obafemi Awolowo: The End of an Era?* (Ile Ife, 1988), pp 18–63; M Okoye, *The Beard of Prometheus* (Bristol, 1965); *A Letter to Dr. Nnamdi Azikiwe: A Dissent Remembered* (Enugu, 1979); T Falola, *Development Planning and Decolonization in Nigeria* (Florida, 1996); *Reforms and Economic Modernization in Nigeria* (Kent: Kent University Press, 2004).

8. EO Awa, *Federal Government in Nigeria* (Berkeley, 1964); "The Place of Ideology in Nigerian Politics," *African Review: Journal of African Politics, Development and International Affairs, Vol.4, nos.3,* 1974, pp 359–380.

9. O Aluko, "Foreign Service," *Quarterly Journal of Administration, nos.5,* 1970, pp 33–52; "The Organisation and Administration of the Nigerian Foreign Service," *Ife International Relations, Occasional Papers, 1,* July 1981, pp 1–39; AHM Kirk-Greene, "The New African Administrator," *Journal of Modern African Studies, vol. x, no.1,* 1972, pp 93–107; "Diplomacy and Diplomats: The Formation of Foreign Service Cadres in Black Africa," in K Ingham, (ed.) *Foreign Relations of African States:* Colston Paper no.25 (London, 1974); CS Phillips, *The Development of Nigerian Foreign Policy* (Evanston, 1964).

10. BJ Dudley, "Marxism and Political Change in Nigeria," *The Nigerian Journal of Economic and Social Studies, vol.6, no.2,* 1964, pp 161–162; JD

Omer-Cooper, "Nigeria, Marxism and Social Progress: An Historical Perspective," *NJESS, vol.6, no.2,* 1964, p 138; KWJ Post, "Nationalism and Politics in Nigeria: A Marxist Approach," *NJESS, vol.6, no.2,* 1964.

11. R Apthorpe, "Opium of the State—Some Remarks on Law and Society in Nigeria," *The Nigerian Journal of Economic and Social Studies, vol.6, no.2,* July 1964, pp 139–154; RS Bhambri, "Marxist Economic Doctrines and their Relevance to Problems of Economic Development of Nigeria," *The Nigerian Journal of Economic and Social Studies, vol.6, no.2,* July 1964, p 196.

12. EEG Iweriebor, *Radical Politics in Nigeria, 1945 -1950: The Significance of the Zikist Movement* (Zaria, 1996). HI Tijani, "Communists and the Nationalist Movement," in T Falola, (ed.) *Nigeria in the Twentieth Century* (Durham, 2002).

13. R Melson, "Marxists in the Nigerian labour movement: A case study in the failure of ideology," PhD Political Science, MIT, 1967; WH Friedland, "Organizational Chaos and Political Potentials," *Africa Report, vol.10, no.6,* June 1965; PF Gonidec, "The Development of Trade Unionism in Black Africa," *Bulletin of the Inter-African Labour Institute, vol. x, no.2,* May 1963; K Laybourn, *The Rise of Socialism in Britain* (Sutton, 1997); GE Lichtblau, "The Dilemma of the ICFTU," *Africa Report op.cit;* "The Communist Labour Offensive in Former Colonial Countries," *Industrial and Labor Relations Review, vol.15, no.3,* April 1962; D Nelkin, "The Search for Continental Unity," *Africa Report op.cit;* M Roberts, "African Trade Unionism in Transition," *The World Today, vol.17, no.10,* October 1961; I Zakharia, & C Magigwana, "The Trade Unions and the Political Scene in Africa," *World Marxist Review,* December 1964.

14. H Adi, "West Africans and the Communist Party in 1950s"; *ICS Postgraduate Seminar,* February, 1994; "West African Students and West African Nationalism in Britain, 1900–1960," PhD History Thesis, University of London, 1994; "The Communist Movement in West Africa," *Science and Society, vol.61, No. 1,* Spring 1997, pp 94–97; S Howe, *Anticolonialism in British Politics: The Left and the end of Empire, 1918–1964* (Oxford, 1993); J Callaghan, "The Communists and the colonies: Anti-imperialism between the Wars," in A Geoff et al (eds.) *Opening the Books: Essays in the Social and Cultural History of Communism* (London, 1995).

15. R Hyam, (ed.) *British Documents on the end of Empire: The Labour Government and the End of Empire, 1945-1951, Part II, Economic and International Relations* (London, 1992), pp 297-379.

16. D Goldsworthy, (ed.) *British Documents on the end of Empire: The Conservative Government and the end of Empire, Part 1,* (London, 1994), pp xxxvii, xxxvii, and xxxix.

17. A Oyebade, "Feeding America's War Machine: The United States and Economic Expansion in West Africa During World War II," *African Economic History,* 26, 1998, pp 119–140.

18. AB Davidson, & SV Mazov, (eds.) *Russia and Africa: Documents and Materials, XVIII Century—1960* (Moscow, 1999); M Matusevich, *No*

Easy Row for a Russian Hoe: Ideology and Pragmatism in Nigeria-Soviet Relations, 1960–1991 (Trenton, 2003).

19. ET Wilson, *Russia and Black Africa before World War II* (London, 1974).

20. A Bello, *My Life* (Cambridge, 1962); O Awolowo, *Awo: An Autobiography of Chief Obafemi Awolowo* (Cambridge, 1961); A Enahoro, *A Fugitive Offender: An Autobiography* (London, 1962); BS Smith, *But Always as Friends* (London, 1964). A more general aid to political biography of African nationalists and leaders is J Grace & J Laffin, *Fontana Dictionary of Africa Since 1960* (London, 1991).

21. M Amechi, *The Forgotten Heroes of Nigerian Independence* (Onitsha, 1985); I Nzimiro, *On Being a Marxist: The Nigerian Marxist and the Nigerian Revolution, 1945-1952* (Zaria, 1983); KO Mbadiwe, *Rebirth of a Nation* (Enugu, 1991); A Osita, "A Call For Revolution and the Forgotten Heroes: The Story of the Zikist Revolution of 1948," *Journal of the Association of Francophone Studies, Vol; 1,no.1,* 1990; HO Davies, *Memoirs* (Ibadan, 1989); H Foot, *A Start in Freedom* (London, 1964).

22. N Azikiwe, *Ideology for Nigeria: Capitalism, Socialism or Welfarism?* (Lagos, 1980), p 56; *My Odyssey* (London, 1970). A critique of Azikiwe's writings and views can be found in A Igwe, *ZIK: A Philosopher of Our Time* (Enugu, 1992).

23. T Clark, *A Right Honourable Gentleman—Abubakar from the Black Rock* (London, 1991). S Epelle, (ed.) *Nigeria Speaks: Speeches of Alhaji Sir Abubakar Tafawa Balewa* (Ikeja, 1964), pp 9–10.

NOTES TO CHAPTER TWO

1. H Grimal, Decolonization: The British, French, Dutch and Belgian Empires, 1919–1963 (Boulder, 1978), pp 17–18. RJC Young, Postcolonialism: An Historical Introduction (Massachusetts/Oxford, 2001), pp 1–12; 159–181; 217–273.

2. A Mayer, *Wilson vs. Lenin: Political Origins of the New Diplomacy, 1917–1918* (New York, 1967), pp 245–266. Young, *Postcolonialism*, pp 113–134. By way of exemplifying the shift from inspiration to disillusionment, historians recount how in 1919, a young Ho Chi Minh, then living in Paris, requested a meeting with President Wilson to present an anti-colonial, nationalist petition of "The Claims of the People of Annam." Rebuffed, that same year Ho took up Marxism-Leninism as revolutionary strategy for a struggle for Vietnamese independence from France. HT Hue-Tam, *Radicalism and the Origins of the Vietnamese Revolution* (Cambridge, Mass., 1992), pp 68–69.

3. M Fainsord, "Soviet Communism," *International Encyclopedia of Social Sciences* (London, 1999), p 105.

4. R Albertini, "The Impact of the Two World Wars on the Decline of Colonialism," in *The End of the European Empire: Decolonisation after World War II,* T Smith, (ed), (London, 1975), pp 3–19.

5. E Friedman, "Maoism, Titoism, Stalinism: Some origins and consequences of the Maoist theory of the socialist transition," in M Seldon, & V Lippit, (eds.) *The Transition to Socialism in China* (New York, 1982).

6. Ibid.

7. J Hatch, "The Decline of British Power in Africa," in T Smith, (ed.) *The End of the European Empire: Decolonization after World War II* (London, 1975), pp 72–100.

8. Ibid.

9. Hatch, Ibid.

10. R Albertini, "The Impact of the Two World Wars on the Decline of Colonialism," in *The End of the European Empire: Decolonization after World War II*, T Smith, (ed), (London, 1975), pp 3–19.

11. JFA Ajayi, & AE Ekoko, "Transfer of Power in Nigeria: Its Origins and Consequences," in P Gifford, & W Louis, (eds.) *Decolonization and African Independence; the Transfers of Power, 1960–1980* (New Haven, Yale, 1988), pp 245–269.

12. Ibid, p 246.

13. HI Tijani, "Communists and the nationalist movement," in T Falola (ed.) *Nigeria in the Twentieth Century* (Durham, 2002), p 293–313; "McCarthyism in colonial Nigeria: The ban on the employment of Communists," in A Oyebade (ed.) *The Foundations of Nigeria* (Trenton, 2003), pp 645–668.

14. CP/CENT/INT/24/04: "Draft discussion of the leadership and personnel of the Nigerian trade union and national movement," November 15, 1951, National Museum of Labour History Archives (NMLHA), Warwick, England.

15. CP/CENT/INT/24/04: Eze (Lagos) to Dafe (London), December 5, 1951, NMLHA, Warwick, England.

16. CP/CENT/INT/20/01: The Nigerian Commission 1950–1953, NMLHA.

17. S Pierson, *Marxism and the origins of socialism: The struggle for a new consciousness* (Ithaca, 1973).

18. E Friedman, "Maoism, Titoism, Stalinism: Some origins and consequences of the Maoist theory of the socialist transition," p 189.

19. CP/CENT/INT/19/01: Nigeria 1952–1957, NMLHA.

20. *Nigeria Socialist Review,* No.1, Editorial notes, February 29, 1952.

NOTES TO CHAPTER THREE

1. FO371/80125/1017/4: "Note on the Aims, Strategy and Procedure of the Communists in Africa," May 1, 1950, PRO, London; "AMCONGEN, Lagos, to Secretary of State: Communism in Nigeria, 1949," File 848L.00B/9–2849, National Archives and Record Administration, College Park (NARA), Maryland, USA; PSF Box 254–64: "Soviet Bloc Capabilities through mid-1953," Harry S. Truman Library (HTL), Independence, Missouri; TT Hammonds, and R Farrell, (eds.) *The Anatomy of Communist Take-overs* (New Haven, 1975).

2. See, M Halpern, "The Middle East and North Africa," pp 319–320; Lewis, W.H. "sub-Saharan Africa," pp 370–371, in CE Black, and TP Thornton, (eds.) *Communism and Revolution*. CO 537/4731: Communism in West Africa—memorandum by RES Yeldham, March 16, 1949.
3. WH Lewis, *sub-Saharan Africa*, p 372.
4. Ibid, p 383; R Joseph, *Radical Nationalism in Cameroon: Social Origins of the UPC Rebellion* (London, 1973).
5. CO537/5263: A Survey of Communism in Africa 1950, PRO, London, pp 3–60.
6. "Amcongen, Lagos, to D.O.S.: Communist activity in Nigeria—File 745H.001/1–656, NARA, College Park, Maryland, p 1. The British TUC was also of the same view. See Mss292/File 966.3/2: W.F.T.U. activities in Nigeria n.d. (probably late 1950), TUC Registry Files 1948–51, Modern Record Centre, The University of Warwick, Warwick, England.
7. JS Coleman, *Nigeria: Background to Nationalism* (Berkeley, 1958); FU Anyiam, *Men and Matters in Nigerian Politics, 1934–1958* (Lagos, 1958); R Sklar, *Nigerian Political Parties: Power in an Emergent African Nation* (Princeton, 1963); GO Olusanya, "The Zikist Movement: A Study in Political Radicalism," *Journal of Modern African Studies*, vol.4, 1966; *The Second World War,* pp 36–37, 116; O Aluko, "Politics of Decolonisation in British West Africa, 1945–1960," in JFA Ajayi, and M Crowder, (eds.) *History of West Africa, vol. II,* (London, 1974); A Osita, "A call for revolution and the forgotten heroes: The story of the Zikist revolution of 1948," *Journal of the Association of Francophone Studies,* vol.1, no.1, 1990.
8. G Padmore, *Communism or Pan-Africanism?;* A Ajala, *Pan-Africanism: Evolution;* PO Esedebe, *Pan-Africanism: The Idea and Movement;* L Spitzer and L Denzer, "I.T.A. Wallace Johnson and the West African Youth League," *Journal of African Historical Studies*, vol. 6, nos.3–4, 1973; SKB Asante, *Pan-African Protests: West Africa and the Italo-Ethiopian Crisis, 1934–1941* (London, 1977); GO Olusanya, *The West African Students' Union and the Politics of Decolonisation, 1925–1958* (Ibadan, 1982); H Adi, and M Sherwood, *The 1945 Manchester Pan-African Congress Revisited* (London, 1995); R Okonkwo, *Protest Movements in Lagos, 1908–1930* (New York, 1995).
9. JS Coleman, *Nigeria*, p 249.
10. Ibid.
11. N Azikiwe, *Ideology for Nigeria: Capitalism, Socialism or Welfarism?* (Lagos, 1980).
12. Awa quite agreed with this position. See, EO Awa, "The Place of Ideology in Nigerian Politics," *African Review,* p 369.
13. Pearce has briefly narrated that Azikiwe's visit to College of Good Hope, Caux-sur-Montreux, Switzerland in November 1949, was partly instrumental in his change of heart from violence to "constitutionalism and peaceful means." See his "Governors, Nationalists, and the Constitution in Nigeria, 1935–1951," *Journal of Imperial and Commonwealth History,*

vol.ix, no.3, May 1981, p 304. His view that nationalists did not influence constitutional changes is inaccurate and suspect.

14. N Azikiwe, *Ideology for Nigeria: Capitalism, Socialism or Welfarism?* (Lagos, 1980), p 90.

15. Ibid, p 91. One of the leading Marxists of the period, Mokwugo Okoye, notes that: "it was not until the end of the World War II . . . that the ideas of the revolution spread like prairie fire and captivated the proletarian masses . . ." See, M Okoye, *A Letter to Dr. Nnamdi Azikiwe: A Dissent Remembered* (Enugu, 1979), p 1.

16. Azikiwe, *Ideology for Nigeria*, p 91.

17. Ibid.

18. Ibid.

19. Ibid.

20. Ibid.

21. Ibid, pp 91–92. Nduka Eze, "A Discourse on Violence and Pacifism as Instruments of Struggle for Freedom," *West African Pilot*, May 13, 1950. Thanks to my friend Dr. Phillip Zachernuk (Dalhousie University, Halifax, Canada) for making a copy available to me.

22. The organisation was formed in 1946 without the participation of Azikiwe himself. See, CO537/7171: The Zikist Movement, 1950; CO537/5807: R.J. Vile to J.K. Thompson, April 27, 1950, PRO, London.

23. CO537/7171: "The Zikist Movement."

24. CO537/3694: "Political Summary of Nigeria, 1950," PRO, London.

25. Ibid. In fact, the government accused the Zikists for the escalation of the Enugu colliery miners' strike in November 1949. The Fitzgerald Commission's Report however remarked that the incident was purely an industrial issue between the management of the colliery and the miners. To them, there was no trace of external influence. See, Report of the Commission into the Disorders in the Eastern Provinces of Nigeria, no.256, (HMSO: London, 1950).

26. See, Raji Abdallah's letter to the Zikists and his northern brethren in West African Pilot, February 25, 1949; CO537/3649: Nigeria-Political Summary October -November, 1948, PRO, pp 4-5.

27. Ibid. See Chapters Three and Four in this study for further accounts of Zikists activities.

28. African Echo, April 6, 1949. CO 537/4727: Nigeria political summary, May 1949.

29. Daily Mirror, March 8, 1950. CO 537/5801: Sir James Macpherson to Mr. Griffiths on the arrests of Zikist members, March 25, 1950, PRO. I Nzimiro, On Being a Marxist is an in-depth account of his role during the period. An analysis of newspaper reports of the sedition trial is contained in EEG Iweriebor, Radical Politics in Nigeria, pp 171-209.

30. CO537/5807: R.J. Vile to J.K. Thompson, April 27th 1950, PRO, London.

31. CO583/302/13: Macpherson to Secretary of State for colonies, February 25, 1950, PRO, London.

32. Daily Times, March 14, 1950.

33. CO583/302/13: Macpherson to Secretary of State.
34. Ibid. Iweriebor has used newspaper reports to narrate events during the Kaduna conference. See *Radical Politics*, pp 231-235. He is however silent about the recruitment of some members as "assassins" to carry out the 1950 plot, neither is he aware about Okoye's appointment as the leader of the group. For details see HI Tijani, "Communists and the Nationalist Movement," T Falola, (ed.) Nigeria in the Twentieth Century (Durham, 2002).
35. Daily Telegraph (London), July 21, 1950.
36. Government Notices No. 21, Volume 37, April 13th, 1950. See, M Okoye, A Letter to Dr. Nnamdi Azikiwe, p 30.
37. NSUDIV8/1/305: Why Government Banned the Zikist Movement, April 29, 1950, National Archives Enugu (NAE), Nigeria; Government Notices nos.21, vol.37, April 1950, Nigerian Secretariat, Lagos, Nigeria.
38. Ibid. Also, CO 537/4727: Nigeria political summary on tensions in the Zikist movement and increasing influence of NYM, May 1949, PRO. OYO Prof. 1/4957: Secretary Western Province to the Resident, Oyo province-"Zikist Movement in Nigeria 1950" Extraordinary Gazette, no.13, April 1950, NAI. Attempts to eulogise and propagate this idea were made through newspaper article by Nduka Eze. In May 13, 1950 he published "A discourse on violence and pacifism as instruments of the struggle for freedom" in Labour Champion. He justified violence as the best recipe for the overthrow of British rule in Nigeria.
39. See, M Okoye, A Letter to Dr.Nnamdi Azikiwe, p 56. The infiltration of the bourgeoisie group was one of the steps taken by the Marxists in Nigeria to make themselves relevant in colonial politics. This perhaps explains why they returned to the major political parties in 1954/55 in order to renew their struggle. See, HI Tijani, "McCarthyism in Colonial Nigeria: The Ban on the Employment of Communists," A Oyebade, (ed.) The Foundations of Nigeria (Trenton, 2003), pp 661-663.
40. CO968/353: Benion to Shaw and Hujisman, November 1950, PRO, London.
41. DEFE82/51: Undesirable Publication Policy, June 10, 1953. For instance, in 1953 Samuel Ikoku was arrested and jailed for being in possession of Nigerian Socialist Review See H Adi, "West African" p 256; "AMCONGEN, Lagos to Department of State: Communism in Nigeria Today," File747H.0018-1453, August 14, 1953, NARA, College Park, Maryland, p 4.
42. NSUDIV8/1/305: "Why Government Banned the Zikist Movement,"
43. "AMCONGEN, Lagos to Department of State: Zikist Movement," File 848L.00/7-1047, July 10, 1947, College Park, Maryland.
44. Ibid.
45. Nigerian Spokesman Editorial, September 3, 1946.
46. Okoye, M. A Letter to Dr. Nnamdi Azikiwe, pp 14-15.
47. CO537/3649: Nigeria-Political Summary, October-November 1948, PRO, London.
48. Ibid, pp 2-3.
49. Ibid, p 3.

50. NSUDIV 8/1/305: Why the Government banned the Zikist Movement, May 29 1950, Appendix 2, NAE, emphasis in original.
51. CO537/3649: Nigeria-Political Summary, p 3.
52. Ibid.
53. Ibid, pp 3-4.
54. Ibid.
55. NSUDIV8/1/305: "Why Government Banned the Zikist Movement."
56. Ibid.
57. Ibid.
58. CO537/7171: "The Zikist Movement, 1949," PRO, London; M Amechi, The Forgotten Heroes of Nigerian Independence, p 91. Amechi was the Assistant Secretary-General of Eze's Nigeria National Federation of Labour in 1950, as well as Assistant Secretary, Public Utility Board Staff Union.
59. CO537/7171: "The Zikist Movement;" see Ndulue's letter to Labour MP Fenner Brockway enclosed.
60. Ibid.
61. Ibid.
62. Ibid.
63. "Keeler to Department of State: Communism in Nigeria-August 14, 1953," File745H.001/8-1453, College Park, Maryland, p 4.
64. Ibid.
65. Ibid.
66. M Ojike, The Road to Freedom (London, 1949).

NOTES TO CHAPTER FOUR

1. CP/CENT/INT/50/03: "Marxist" Groups in Nigeria—Draft for Commission, August 4, 1953, National Museum of Labour History Archive (NMLH), Manchester.
2. Ibid.
3. Ibid.
4. CP/CENT/INT/50/05: The Communist Party (Nigeria and Cameroons), Ibadan, to, The Executive Committee, The Communist Party, London, March 19, 1951, NMLH, p 1.
5. CP/CENT/INT/25/01: Statement Issued by The League, Lagos, Nigeria, October 1951, NMLH, p 1.
6. Ibid.
7. Ibid.
8. CP/CENT/INT/50/05: Idise Dafe—Report on Visit to Nigeria, n.d. (probably 1951 or 1952), NMLH, p 4.
9. CP/CENT/INT/550/05: Amaefule Ikoro to Communist Party of Great Britain, 1951, NMLH.
10. Ibid, p 1.
11. Ibid.
12. CP/CENT/INT/50/05: Peoples Committee for Independence—Circular Letter No.1/52, February 22, 1952, NMLH.

13. Ibid, p 1; CP/CENT/INT/25/01: Peoples Committee for Independence, Lagos, to Guiseppe Di Vittorio and Louis Saillant (WFTU), Paris, May 7, 1952, p 1.

14. Ibid, p 1; and, CP/CENT/INT/50/05: Ikoku, S.G. *et.al* Manifesto of the . . . Party of Nigeria and the Cameroons, n.d. NMLH. There is need to set the record straight here. Chukwudolue Orhakamalu was not the first secretary of the UWPP as suggested by Maxim Matusevich (See "*Crying Wolf: Early Nigerian Reactions to the Soviet Union, 1960–1966*," in Falola, T. (ed.) *Nigeria in the Twentieth Century*, (Durham, 2002), p 710. According to the records of the Communist Party cited above, he became secretary of the CPN after Uche Omo's term in 1952.

15. CP/CENT/INT/50/03: "Marxist" Groups in Nigeria, p 3.

16. CP/CENT/INT/24/04: Nigeria—Report for January 1956, p 13.

17. Ibid. Also, CP/CENT/INT/50/03: Marxist groups, p 9.

18. CP/CENT/INT/24/04: Nigeria, p 13.

19. Ibid.

20. CP/CENT/INT/25/01: Peoples Committee; Also, CP/CENT/INT/25/01: Ikoku, S.G. "Report on the trade union movement in Nigeria," autumn 1951.

21. Editorial Comments: *Nigerian Socialist Review, no.1,* February 29, 1952.

22. Ibid, p 1.

23. Ibid.

24. Ibid.

25. Kolakowski, L. *Main Currents of Marxism—Volume 3*, (Oxford, 1981).

26. *Nigerian Socialist Review*, no. 2, March 14, 1952, p 2.

27. *Nigerian Socialist Review*, no.1, p 1–2.

28. Ibid.

29. *Nigerian Socialist Review*, no. 2, p 2.

30. Mmaba, C.O. "A Young Socialist at Work," *Nigerian Socialist Review*, no.1; Anagbogbu, M. "Unfurling the banner of struggle for Independence and Socialism," *Nigerian Socialist Review*, no.2, p 2.

31. Editorial comment, *Nigerian Socialist Review*, no.2.

32. Anagbogu, M. "Unfurling the banner," *Nigerian Socialist Review*, no.2.

33. CP/CENT/INT/50/03: Marxist Groups in Nigeria, p 4.

34. Ibid, p 5.

35. Ibid, pp 5–6.

36. CP/CENT/INT/50/03: Marxist Groups in Nigeria, p 4.

37. CP/CENT/INT/48/01: What Next in Nigeria?—1954, p 18.

38. Ibid.

39. Ibid.

40. "Africa—Communism: Communist in the Federation of Nigeria," 1961, p 1, Lyndon Baines Johnson Presidential Library, University of Texas-Austin, Texas, USA.

NOTES TO CHAPTER FIVE

1. CP/CENT/INT/24/04: "Draft Discussion Document," November 1951, NMLHA, p 3. For a detailed theoretical reconstruction see RJC Young, *Postcolonialism: An Historical Introduction* (Massachusetts/Oxford, 2001), pp 217–230, 239–242, 274–292. On general history of the CPGB, see, N Branson, *History of the Communist Party of Great Britain, 1927–1941* (London, 1987); *History of the Communist Party of Great Britain, 1941–1951* (London, 1997).

2. CP/CENT/INT/50/3: "Marxist" Groups in Nigeria—Draft for Commission, August 4, 1953, NMLHA; CO537/5807: R.J. Vile to J.K. Thompson, pp 1–24; also, "AMCONGEN, Lagos to Department of State: The Case of Nduka Eze-Communist Leader in Nigeria," File745H.00/8–251, NARA, p 1. At the peak of his career, he became the Action Group chairman for Asaba District in 1956. One can conclude that this was largely because of the success of government anti-communist measures. Nduka Eze died however in December 1995. Access to his private papers, if any, would illuminate our knowledge about his life.

3. Mss292/File 966.3/2, Nduka Eze to Mr. Kemmis, Secretary TUC Colonial Advisory Committee, June 7, 1949, TUC Registry Files 1948–51, Modern Record Centre, The University of Warwick, Warwick, England.

4. Ibid. Curry to Tewson, March 23, 1949; Curry to H.B. Kemmis, June 24, 1949.

5. Ibid. Curry to Tewson, March 23, 1949.

6. CO537/3649: "Nigeria-Political Summary," p 2.

7. CP/CENT/INT/24/04: "Draft Discussion Document."

8. Ibid.

9. " . . . The Case of Nduka Eze . . ." File745H.00/8–251, In fact, Eze and some ex-Zikists had by 1951, renounced Zikism for a more specific ideology of revolutionary socialism. See, R Sklar, *Nigerian Political Parties*, p 81.

10. CP/CENT/INT/24/04: Draft Discussion Document. Teachings and lectures were based on CPGB document, "Essentials of Communist Theory: A Three Lesson Syllabus." See, CP/CENT/ED/1/4: "Essentials . . ." September 5, 1943.

11. CAB134/1353: Communist Penetration—Africa Report, 1958, PRO, London. More information about the activities of the Czechs is yet to be unfolded due to non-availability of records.

12. "The Case of Nduka Eze," File745H.00/8–251, NARA, p 2.

13. CO537/4632: Nigeria—Political Summary. Folarin Coker later reneged on communism. See his letter to Miss Darlow of *The Guild*, University College, Exeter, United Kingdom.

14. "The Case of Nduka Eze" File745H.00/8–251, NARA, p 2.

15. Ibid.

16. Ibid, p 3.

17. Ibid.
18. Ibid.
19. Ibid.
20. Ibid.
21. Ibid.
22. Ibid.
23. Ibid.
24. "Fortnightly Review: November 4–17, 1951, File745H.00/11–1951;"Fort-nightly Review: July 2–14, 1951, File745H.00/7–1751;"Fortnightly Review: August 12–25, 1951, File745.008/8–2751; and "Fortnightly Newsletter, December 16–29, 1951, File745H.00/12–2951; NARA.
25. CONSUL, Lagos to Department of State: Communist Fund for Nigerian Labor—August 19, 1951," File745H.001/1–1951, NARA.
26. CP/CENT/INT/25/01: Report on the Trade Union Movement in Nigeria, autumn 1951, NMLHA, p 7.
27. Ibid.
28. Ibid.
29. Ibid, p 8.
30. W Ananaba, *The Trade Union Movement in Nigeria* (London, 1969), pp 141, 298, 300 and 322; R Cohen, *Labour and Politics in Nigeria* (2nd Edition, London, 1981), p 79; MA Tokunboh, *Labour Movement in Nigeria, Past and Present* (Lagos, 1985), pp 50–58.
31. "Communist Fund for Nigerian Labor Union," File745H.001/1–1951, NARA. Also, see, *Daily Mirror* (London), January 18, 1951. W Ananaba, *The Trade Union Movement in Nigeria,* pp 141–155.
32. "Review of Recent Labor Developments in Nigeria—August 8, 1958," File845H.06/8–857, NARA, p 3.
33. "The Case of Nduka Eze," p 1.
34. Ibid.
35. "Recent Labor Developments" File845H.06/8–857, NARA, p 3; EA Egboh, "The Early Years of Trade Unionism in Nigeria," *Africa Quarterly,* Volume viii, no1, April-June 1968, pp 59–69; Richard Sklar cannot be right when he referred to Gogo Chu Nzeribe as "a relatively unknown candidate at the 1953 All-Nigerian Trade Union Movement conference." See R Sklar, *Nigerian Political Parties,* p 81 and 529.
36. "Recent Labor Developments," File845H.06/8–857, NARA.
37. Ibid.
38. Ibid.
39. Ibid.
40. Mss292/File 966.3/3: Footnotes on visit of Nigerian Ministers—Okotie-Eboh and C. Okwu, July 2, 1957, TUC Registry Files 1951–60, Modern Record Centre, Warwick.
41. "Recent Labor Developments," File845H.06/8–857. Perhaps one can argue that this was purely a trade union tactics.
42. See, M Sherwood, *Kwame Nkrumah: The Years Abroad, 1935 -1947* (Legon, 1996), pp 125–127.

43. Ibid, p 153. We must state that Samuel Akpata is not the same as Ayo Akpata, who later became an Assistant Registrar, Student Affairs, University of Ibadan in 1963.
44. CO1039/34: Nigerian Council of Ministers Miscellaneous Papers 1954, PRO, London.
45. Sherwood, M. *Kwame Nkrumah,* p 128. We must acknowledge that further study on Dr. Bankole Akpata still need to be done to unearth his role in Ghana and Nigeria during the period.
46. HO Davies, *Memoirs* (Ibadan, 1989). GO Olusanya, *The West African Students' Union and the Politics of Decolonisation, 1925–1958* (Ibadan, 1982). H Adi, "Anti-Colonial Activity in Britain," in Toyin Falola, (ed.) *Nigeria in the Twentieth Century,* pp 315–332.
47. "AMCONSUL, Lagos to Department of State: Development of two Leftist Groups—October 25, 1951," File745H.00/10–2351, NARA, pp 2–3.
48. Ibid.
49. Ibid.
50. Ibid.
51. For a detailed analysis of this phenomenon, see, R Sklar, *Nigerian Political Parties,* p 115; HI Tijani, "McCarthyism in Colonial Nigeria." RJC Robert, *Postcolonialism,* pp 68 & 227.
52. CP/CENT/INT/24/04: Draft Discussion Document, p 1.
53. Ibid.
54. See, "Letter from Mrs. Freda Gimble, London Women's Parliament Committee," August 29, 1947, Funmilayo Ransome-Kuti Papers (FRK), University of Ibadan, Nigeria. B Awe, (ed.) *Nigerian Women in Historical Perspectives* (Lagos, 1992). C Johnson-Odim & NE Mba, *For Women and the Nation: Funmilayo Ransome-Kuti of Nigeria* (Illinois, 1997), particularly Chapter Six "For Their Freedoms—The International Sphere."
55. See "Letter from Mrs. Freda Gimble, London Women's Parliament Committee," August 29, 1947, Funmilayo Ransome-Kuti Papers (FRK), University of Ibadan, Nigeria.
56. See, "Funmilayo Ransome-Kuti Diary 1952," FRK Papers, University of Ibadan, Nigeria.
57. See, *The Women of Asia and Africa: Documents* (Prague, 1948), and "Funmilayo Ransome-Kuti Diary 1952," FRK Papers, Ibadan.
58. SD/B9: "Passport—Mr. Prime Minister: Statement in Parliament," Government Publications (Lagos, 1964); West African Pilot, August 4, 1954.
59. NE Mba, *Nigerian Women Mobilised* (Berkeley, 1982), pp 142–164. Also, Solanke Paper, Box 73, File 81, August 20, 1952, Gandhi Library, University of Lagos, Nigeria.
60. See "Correspondence, Box 4," FRK Papers, Ibadan.
61. 61. Ibid.
62. Johnson-Odim & Mba, *For Women and the Nation,* pp 137–151.
63. Newspaper reports of the incident can be found in *West African Pilot,* December 30, 1957. *Daily Times* (Nigeria), January 21, 1957. *Daily Service* (Nigeria) March 4, 1958.

64. Ibid.
65. "Communism in Nigeria Today," File 745H.001/8–1453, NARA.

NOTES TO CHAPTER SIX

1. Part of this chapter is published as "McCarthyism in colonial Nigeria: The Ban on the Employment of the Communists," in A Oyebade, (ed.) *The Foundations of Nigeria* (Trenton, 2003), pp 645–668.
2. CO537/6783: Communism in West Africa—Appointments to University Colleges, 1950–1952, (Minutes of September 19, 1950) PRO, London. The background to this was the appointment of two communists in 1948 and 1950 to the teaching staff. J. W. Harris and J. Harper were appointed before the introduction of the vetting system and the Immigration Ordinance of 1950.
3. Ibid. Minutes of November 2, 1951.
4. Ibid. Macpherson to secretary of state for colonies—James Griffiths, May 1, 1951.
5. Ibid. *Manchester Guardian,* October 28, 1956.
6. *The Labour Party Annual Report 1947–1948,* "Campaign Against Communism," (London, 1948), pp 205–208.
7. Ibid, p 208.
8. *TUC Annual Report 1948,* p 305, 532, TUC Collections, University of North London; *House of Commons Debate,* 448, March 15, 1948, pp 1703–1708; Rathbone, R. *Documents on the End of Empire—Ghana, Part II,* (HMSO—London, 1992), p 81.
9. *House of Commons Debate,* p 1703.
10. Ibid, pp 1703–1704.
11. Ibid, pp 1704–1706; 3392–3398.
12. Ibid, p 3424.
13. Ibid, pp 1299–1300.
14. *The Labour Party Annual Report 1947–1948* (London, 1949), p 208.
15. *House of Lords Report,* volume 166, no.10, March 29, 1950.
16. Ibid.
17. Ibid.
18. Rathbone, *British Documents,* p 79.
19. Ibid. Also CO554/371: Sir T. Lloyd to Sir C. Arden-Clarke, January 4, 1954.
20. Ibid.
21. Rathbone, *British Documents,* p 75.
22. Ibid. Also CO554/371: Sir C. Arden-Clarke to W. L. Gorell Barnes, December 4, 1953.
23. Rathbone, *British Documents,* p 82.
24. Ibid. Also PREM 11/1367: Cabinet Memorandum by Lyttelton, February 18, 1954.
25. CO537/6787: Macpherson to secretary of state.
26. Ibid.

27. *Daily Times* (Nigeria); *Daily Service* (Nigeria) and the *West African Pilot* of 20 October 1954. Also, "AMCONGEN, Lagos to the Department of State -Ban on employment of communist in Nigerian Public services," File745H.14/10-2254, October 22, 1954, NARA, College Park, Maryland, USA.

28. *Federation of Nigeria Official Gazette*, No. 57, October 14, 1954 (Government Publishing House, Lagos, 1955).

29. Ibid.

30. See, *Daily Service* (Nigeria), 20 October 1954. For instance, in July 1957, the last colonial chief secretary in Nigeria reiterated that, " . . . this policy [anti-communism] has been followed voluntarily by a number of commercial organisations . . ." See, SO Osoba, "The Economic Foundations of Nigeria's Foreign Policy During the First Republic, 1960—1965," in IA Akinjogbin & SO Osoba, (eds.) *Topics on Nigerian Economic and Social History* (Ile Ife, 1980), p 226.

31. *Daily Service*, 16 October 1954.

32. *West African Pilot*, 15 October 1954.

33. Tijani, "McCarthyism in colonial Nigeria," p 652.

34. "Amcongen . . . to D.O.S.; File 745H.001/1-656, p 2.

35. CO1039/34: Nigerian Council of Ministers Meeting, December 29, 1954, PRO, pp 12-14.

36. "McLauglin to Department of State," File745H.00/6-155, June 1, 1956, NARA, College Park, Maryland, USA.

37. "Amcongen, Lagos to D.O.S.—East Bans Communist Teachers," File745H.00/6-155, June 1, 1955, NARA, College Park, USA.

38. Mss292/File 966.3/6: Anunobi to Tewson, July 27, 1956, *TUC Registry Files*. Anunobi was the national secretary of Mercantile Unions of Nigeria and Cameroons during the period. He was a strong anti-Communist and influential labor leader.

39. Nigeria—Department of Labour Annual Report 1954, (Lagos, 1955), NAI.

40. CP/CENT/INT/48/01: The Working Class Movement and the Need for a Marxist Party, 1954, NMLHA—Manchester, p 16.

41. Ibid.

42. "Hunt to the Department of State," File745H.11/00/11-2157, October 8, 1957, NARA.

43. M Tokunboh, *Labour Movements in Nigeria: Past and Present* (Ibadan, 1985), pp 25-26.

44. Mss292/File 966.3/1: Nigeria, Correspondence/TU Development 1941-8, *TUC Registry File*, University of Warwick, Warwick, England.

45. Ibid

46. Tokunboh, *Labour Movements*, p 26; TUC Colonial Advisory Committee File 1, 1948-49, December 15, 1948, p 2; File 2, 1948-49, April 21, 1949, p 6, *TUC Collections*, University of North London. Other beneficiaries include: T. O. Sangonuga, A. F. A. Awolana, J. W. Wamuo and Abubakar Liman Umaru. See Mss292/File 966.3/4: Winterbottom to Curry, March 4, 1952, *TUC Registry Files*.

47. Tokunboh, *Labour Movement,* p 26. Adio-Moses also benefited from the US Foreign Leader Program in 1951. See Mss292/File 966.3/2: Adio-Moses to Walter Hood, April 27, 1951, *TUC Registry Files.*
48. Ibid. See, *TUC Annual Report (London, 1953),* p 212; *TUC Annual Report (London, 1956),* p 215.
49. CO554/329: Departmental Labour Conferences, Nigeria 1953, PRO.
50. Tokunboh, *Labour Movements,* p 117.
51. Mss292/File 966.3/2: Curry to Tewson, March 23, 1949, *TUC Registry Files.*
52. Tokunboh, *Labour Movements,* p 118.
53. CO537/6704: Oldenboek to James Griffiths, January 8, 1950, PRO, London.
54. Mss292/File 966.3/2: Extracts from letter received from G. B. Lynch, trade union officer, Labour Department, Lagos, Nigeria, January 21, 1950; Lynch to Tewson, May 16, 1950; *TUC Registry Files.*
55. Ibid. Cutting from *The Times* (London), 12 November 1950.
56. CO537/6704: Sir Vincent Tewson to S of S, James Griffiths, November 20, 1950.
57. Ibid.
58. See "Fortnightly Newsletter," File745H.00/2–2552, February 11–23, 1952, NARA, College Park, Maryland, USA.
59. CO537/6704: secretary of state for colonies to O.A.G of Nigeria, the Gold Coast, Gambia and Sierra Leone, December 5, 1950, PRO, London.
60. Ibid. O.A.G to S of S, December 16, 1950.
61. Ibid. Watson to Parry, January 13, 1951.
62. Ibid. James Griffiths to O.A.G (West Africa), January 16, 1951.
63. Ibid. ICFTU delegation to West Africa, 1950/1951, PRO, London. Also, Mss292/File 966.3/3: Extracts from report of visit to Nigeria by Mr.E. Parry, C.E. Ponsonby and Dalgleish, to James Griffith, July-August 1950, *TUC Registry Files,*
64. *West Africa,* Editorial, London, January 27, 1951; Colonial Advisory Committee Minute (CACM), File 2 (1950–51), February 21, 1951,p 7; File 3, May 10, 1951, p 9–11; File 4, September 21, 1951, p 13; *TUC Annual Report 1952,* p 174.
65. See A Carew, "Charles Millard, A Canadian in the International Labour Movement: A Case Study of the ICFTU 1955–1961," *Labour/Le travail* 37 (spring 1996), pp 121–148.
66. CO537/6704: Smith to Gorsuch, April 2, 1951, PRO, London.
67. Ibid. Adio-Moses was appointed as a labor officer in the Western Region in 1958.
68. Mss292/File 966.3/2: Nigeria 1948–51, Walter Hood to Curry, May 7, 1951; *TUC Registry Files.*
69. Mss292/File 966.3/4: Nigeria 1951–53, *TUC Registry Files;* Couzens to Barltrop, November 20, 1951.
70. *The Christian Science Monitor* (Boston) had earlier reported that the basic drive of the ICFTU initiatives "is for free labor group." See July 2, 1956

edition. Also, *Manchester Guardian,* 20 November 1956; TUC Annual Report 1957.

71. *African Labour,* no.5, January 1959,p 2.
72. *TUC Annual Report 1950,* p 155.
73. *TUC Annual Report 1951,* p 223.
74. *TUC Annual Report 1952,* p 154.
75. *TUC Annual Report 1954,* p 228.
76. Mss292/File 966.3/6: Nigeria—Background notes for meeting with Overseas Employers, February 1956, *TUC Registry Files.*
77. CO537/6704: Smith to Gorsuch.
78. D Goldsworthy, (ed.) *British Documents on the end of Empire: The Conservative Government and the End of Empire—Part III,* (HMSO: London, 1994), p 374.
79. Ibid.
80. CO554/1998: Labour Matters in Nigeria, 1957–1959, PRO, London. Also, *West African Pilot,* February 18, 1949.
81. Ibid.
82. CO554/1998: Labour Matters.
83. Ibid.
84. Ibid. Also, see "labour disputes on the M.V. Apapa, 1957–1959," PRO, London; "Board of Inquiry into the Trade Dispute Between the Elder Dempster Lines Limited and the Nigerian Union of Seamen Report, 1959," Government Publications, Lagos, 1959. A special thanks to Ms. Powell, State Department Library, Washington DC, for sending a copy to me.
85. Ibid. Also, "AMCONGEN to the Department of State—Labor dispute involving W. O. Goodluck, secretary of Lever Brothers and Van Der Bergh workers' union," File 845H.062/7–3158, July 31, 1958, NARA; *Daily Times* (Nigeria), July 19, 1958; and *West African Pilot,* July 23, 1958.
86. "AMCONGEN to the Department of State—Status of ANTUF/NCTUN struggle for control of Nigerian Trade Union Movement," File 845H.062/6–2658, June 26, 1958, NARA.
87. CO859/748: Communism in the Colonial Territories and the Trade Unions Memorandum by N.D. Watson, November 9, 1953.
88. Ibid.
89. Ibid. Draft CO record of a discussion between Mr. Lyttelton and the representatives of the TUC and the Overseas Employers Federation, July 12, 1954. Influence and persuasion had been used to resolve the Malaya labor crises earlier in 1954. As the secretary of state for the colonies noted in the draft, "the situation in Malaya had been extremely dangerous a little time ago but the talks which had taken place with Mr. Narayanon and Mr. Ascoli were largely responsible for the happy outcome . . ."
90. "Labor: Further developments in Nigerian Trade Union Movement," File 845H.06/8–2057, August 20, 1957.
91. Ibid.
92. Ibid.
93. Ibid.

94. "AMCONSUL, Lagos to D.O.S.: Conference of Nigerian labor leaders creates new national organization," File 845H.06/3–2359, March 23, 1959, NARA.

95. Ibid. Also, EO Egboh, "Central Trade Unionism in Nigeria (1941–1966)," *Geneve Afrique,* vi, no.2, (1967).

96. "AMCONSUL, Lagos to D.O.S.: Conference of Nigerian Labor Leaders."

97. CP/CENT/INT/20/01: The N.E.P.U. Party of Northern Nigeria—Declaration of Principles, n.d. NMLHA.

98. Ibid.

99. Ibid.

100. *Daily Times* (Nigeria), 11 March 1959.

101. "Constitution of Trade Union Congress of Nigeria," File 845H.062/6–3059, June 30, 1959, NARA, College Park, Maryland. "ICFTU Collections: HD6868—Nigeria (General)," *TUC Collections;* "Superior Strategy Defeats Communist Plan—Nigerian T.U. Movement Finds Unity," *MRA Information Service, vol.8, no.193* (1959) Caux, Switzerland, *TUC Registry Files.*

102. R Sklar, *Nigerian Political Parties: Power in an Emergent African Nation* (Princeton, 1963), p 270.

103. Ibid, pp 270–271.

104. Ibid.

105. Ibid. Also see, A Feinstein, *African Revolutionary: The Life and Times of Nigeria's Aminu Kano* (London, 1992).

106. BJ Dudley, *Parties and Politics in Northern Nigeria* (London, 1968), p 169.

107. R Sklar, *Nigerian Political Parties,* p 372.

108. BJ Dudley, *Parties and Politics in Northern Nigeria* (London, 1968), p 169.

109. Sklar, Nigerian Political Parties, pp 366–376; Dudley Parties and Politics, p 169. Also see, J N Paden, Ahmadu Bello—Sardauna of Sokoto: Values and Leadership in Nigeria (London, 1986).

110. See Dudley, *Parties and Politics;* and A. Feinstein, *African Revolutionary,* for full discussion.

NOTES TO CHAPTER SEVEN

1. A Oyebade, "Feeding the America's War Machine: The United States and Economic Expansion in West Africa during World War II," African Economic History 26 (1998), pp 119-140; S Metz, "American Attitudes Toward Decolonization in Africa," Political Science Quarterly, Fall 84, vol.99 Issue 3, pp 515-533.

2. JPD Dunbabin, The Cold War: The Great Powers and Their Allies (London, 1994), pp 39-40; Full account of Acheson's role is in D Brinkley, Dean Acheson: The Cold War Years, 1953-71 (New Haven, 1994); D Brinkley, Dean Acheson and the making of U.S. Foreign Policy (Basingstoke/New York, 1993).

3. E Schrecker, The Age of McCarthyism: A Brief History with Documents (Boston, 1994), pp 37-38, 151-154;

4. Extant studies in this regard are RB Allen, "Communists should not teach in American Colleges," Educational Forum, vol.13, no.4, May 1949; PL Steinberg, The Great "Red Menace": United States Prosecution of American Communists, 1947-1952 (Connecticut, 1984); E Schrecker, No Ivory Tower: McCarthyism and the Universities (New York, 1986), pp 3-11, 63-83.

5. "Communist Control Act, 1950," Box 3, no.2, Harry S. Truman Presidential Library and Institute, Independence, Missouri. See, https://www.nsa.gov/venona/. JE Haynes & H Klehr, Venona: Decoding Soviet Espionage in America (New Haven, 2000). On Julius and Ethel Rosenberg see J Milton, The Rosenberg File (2nd Edition: New Haven, 1997). P Moynihan, Secrecy: The American Experience (Connecticut, 1998).

6. NSC48, Reel 2, Louis Johnson (Secretary of Defense) to National Security Council, June 10, 1949, Library of Congress, Washington D.C.

7. HI Tijani, "Communists and the Nationalist Movement," pp 293-304.

8. HI Tijani, "McCarthyism in Colonial Nigeria," pp 652-654.

9. See, Louis, R.W. "American anti-colonization and the dissolution of the British Empire," International Affairs, nos. 61, 1985.

10. Henry Kissinger, Diplomacy (London, 1994), p 31.

11. V McKay, Africa in World Politics (London, 1964), p 244.

12. A Kamarck, "The African economy and international trade," The United States and Africa (New York, 1958), p 119.

13. Attempt by Ebere Nwaubani in The United States and Decolonization in West Africa, 1950-1960 (Rochester, 2001), pp 28-55, to explain the significance of West Africa to the United States is unconvincing. His view that officials were not particularly interested or interest was of "lowest priority" is not entirely true. Africa, like any colonial territory was treated within the context of its colonial status. The structure of U.S. Department of State as it relates to African Affairs during the period is not the only yardstick to measure policies or goal, as Nwaubani would want to present. For another view see, ET Dickerson, "A Report of the strategic ports of West Africa," File PSF/E.o.10501, March 1952, Harry S. Truman Presidential Library and Institute, Independence, Missouri, p 4.

14. ET Dickerson, "A Report of strategic ports of West Africa," p 14.

15. McKay, Africa, p 248.

16. Rockefeller Brothers West African Fund, Box 3, 4 and 5, Rockefeller Archives (RF), New York.

17. HI Tijani, "Communists and nationalist movements."

18. Ibid. Ferudi, F. "Diagnosing Disorder: The Anglo-American Management of African Nationalism, 1948-1960," ASAUK Biennial conference 8-10 September 1992, p 12. Adi, H. West Africans in Britain 1900-1960: Nationalism, Pan-Africanism and Communism (London, 1998).

19. "British Colonies of West Africa: policy and information statement," 12 December 1946, File RG59 848K.00, NARA, College Park.

20. Ibid.

21. Ibid.

22. Ibid.
23. Ibid. Byroade, H. Oral History Record, Harry S. Truman Presidential Library and Institute, Independence, Missouri.
24. Childs to DOS: "Political, Economic and Social Survey of Nigeria," File 745H.00/6 951, NARA, College Park.
25. Ibid. Also, see "Summary Discussion," 20 September 1950, File RG59-770.00/9-250F, DOS, NARA, College Park.
26. Bartelt to DOS, RG59-511.45K/11-3051, 30 November 1951, NARA, College Park.
27. HI Tijani, "Communists and the nationalist movement."
28. Jones to DOS: NCTUN Affiliation with ICFTU," 1 October 1958, File 845H.062/10-158, NARA, College Park.
29. Jones to DOS: "ICA Workers' Education Kit," 2 October 1958, File 848H.06/10-258, NARA, College Park.
30. HI Tijani, "McCarthyism in Colonial Nigeria," pp 653-661.
31. Ibid.
32. Ibid.
33. CO936/570: "The Political Scene in tropical Africa," PRO, London. V McKay, Africa, p 345. Daily Telegraph, December 12, 1957.
34. J Henderson, The United States Information Agency (New York, 1969), p 65.
35. HI Tijani, "McCarthyism in colonial Nigeria," pp 647-663.
36. CO536/7542: "Assistance by the USIS on broadcasting in the colonies," PRO, London. "The Nigerian Legislative Council Debate," 13 September 1950, NAI. "Report on Nigerian Trade Unions" File CP/CENT/INT/20/01, 3, National Museum of Labour History and Archives, Manchester, UK.
37. V McKay, Africa, pp 259-260.
38. Am Embassy, London to the Department of State: "Comment by Mining Journal on DMPA Columbium-Tantalum Guaranteed Purchase Program," July 22, 1952.
39. CSO26/10304/S5 vol.1: "Secretary of State for the colonies to the Officer Administering the Government of Nigeria," 29 December 1951, PRO, London.
40. Ibid, p 1.
41. Ibid.
42. See RG 469: "Europe Program Division, 1949-1951, Box 3," August 9, 1950; RG 469: "Memorandum from Allan Smith, Box 47," January 22, 1951, NARA.
43. CSO 26/10304/S5 vol. 1: "Economic Cooperation Act and Bilateral Agreements," p 2.
44. Ibid, p 3.
45. Ibid. See attached Circular 253/52 "Mutual Security Act: Exemption from taxation of the United States expenditure under the Act," p 1.
46. Ibid. See enclosed "Agreed Minute" March 15, 1952.

47. NIGCOAL: 3-21: Correspondence of Nigeria Coal Corporation 1950-1953, NAI. Also, Nigeria Yearbook, 1953 (Government Publication, Lagos, Nigeria).
48. Ibid. "Overseas Development Pool Memo," 29 September 1952, pp 1-2.
49. Detail about projects carried out in other parts of West Africa is contained in Nwaubani, E. The United States and Decolonization in West Africa, Chapters Three and Four. Regrettably, Nwabauni did not use PRO documents nor did he mention the Enugu Colliery and Kano-Lamy projects under the ECA/MSA. This gap is filled on these pages.
50. A detailed account is contained in R Ovendale, British Defence Policy since 1945 (Manchester, 1994).
51. FO 371/118677: B. Salt (Washington D.C.) to J.A.H. Watson, 11 June 1956; Sir G. Jebb (Paris) to S. Lloyd, 31 October 1956, PRO, London.
52. Ibid. See, J Kent, "Anglo-French colonial co-operation 1939-1949," Journal of Imperial and Commonwealth History, vol. xvii, no.1, October 1988, pp 55-89; DEK, Amenumey, The Ewe Unification Movement: A Political History (Accra, 1989).
53. CO 537/7148: Anglo-French Relations in West Africa, 1951, PRO, London.
54. Ibid, pp 8-9.
55. Ibid.
56. Ibid.
57. CO 537/6555: Griffiths to governors of British colonies in West Africa, 13 March, 1950; Henderson to chief secretary, West African Council, Accra, 16 April, 1950, PRO, London.

NOTES TO CHAPTER EIGHT

1. CAB134/1355: Cabinet—Africa (Official) Committee: NATO Report on Communist Penetration in Africa—Note by the Foreign Office, May 27, 1959, p 2; CAB134/1355: Cabinet—Africa (Official) Committee: Soviet Bloc Economic Offensive in Africa -Note by the Foreign Office, October 26, 1959, PRO, London.
2. FO371/137972: Foreign Office Memorandum—Africa: The Next Ten Years, November 23, 1959. See DJ Morgan, *The Official History of Colonial Development, Volume Three*, pp 211–266.
3. See Toyin Falola and Julius Ihonvbere (eds.) *Nigeria and the International Capitalist System* (Boulder: Rienner Publication, 1989). Understanding official mind is better documented in Ronald Hyam and William R. Louis (eds.) *The conservative government and the end of empire, 1957–1964: Parts 1 and 2* (London: HMSO-London, 2000). Frank Heinlein, *British government policy and decolonisation, 1945–1963: Scrutinising the official mind* (London: Frank Cass, 2002).
4. For a background discussion of the period, see DJ Morgan, *The Official History: Volume Three*, pp 84–91.

5. CAB134/1353: Cabinet—Africa (Official) Committee: Future Constitutional Development in the Colonies—East and West Africa: Notes by the Secretaries, January 6, 1959, p 3.

6. CAB134/1353: Cabinet—Africa (Official) Committee: Prospects for the African Territories for which the Colonial Office is Responsible—Memorandum by the Colonial Office, January 1959, paragraph 24. Azikiwe later became the first President of independent Nigerian nation. He was the founder and leader of the NCNC and the West African Pilot.

7. Ibid, paragraph 25–27.

8. Ibid. Ojedokun, O. "The Anglo-Nigerian Entente and its Demise, 1960–1962," *Journal of Commonwealth Political Studies,* Volume ix, Number 3, November 1971, pp 210–233. Balewa was a deputy leader of the NPC and a strong believer in anti-leftist policy. He emerged as the leader of government business and later prime minister of Nigeria on October 1, 1960.

9. CAB134/1353: Cabinet—Africa (Official) Committee: Prospects for the African Territories, paragraph 27.

10. CAB134/1353: Cabinet—Africa (Official) Committee: Minutes of Meeting—The Next Ten Years in Africa—West Africa, January 21, 1959, p 5.

11. Their reservation might have being informed by Azikiwe's support of a "neutralist" foreign policy in 1959. See *Daily Times,* August 22, 1959; for details about foreign policy and the 1959 election campaign, see, CS Phillips, *The Development of Nigerian Foreign Policy* (Evanston, 1964), pp 14–24; KWJ Post, *The Nigeria Federal Election of 1959,* p 311.

12. CAB134/1355: Cabinet—Africa (Official) Committee: NATO Report, p 2.

13. Ibid.

14. Quoted from CAB134/1354: The Political Scene in Tropical Africa, November 1958, PRO, London.

15. Ibid. Also, O Aluko, *Ghana and Nigeria 1957—1970: A Study in Inter-African Discord,* (London, 1976).

16. CAB134/1354: The Political Scene in Tropical Africa, p 4.

17. Ibid, p 2.

18. FO371/146827: Problems Involved in Establishing and Maintaining Diplomatic Relations with Soviet Union, January 12, 1960.

19. Ibid.

20. FO371/146832: Meeting of the Prime Minister of Nigeria with the Secretary of State for Foreign and Commonwealth Affairs and the Colonial Secretary at the Foreign Office, November 29, 1960.

21. Ibid.

22. Ibid.

23. DO 35/10489, "Letter from Sir J Robertson to Sir H Poynton on Alhaji Sir Abubakar Tafawa Balewa," Minute by BJ Greenhill, February 19, 1960, PRO; For details about the special relationship between Balewa and Robertson see, Sir James Robertson, *Transition in Africa: From Direct Rule to Independence—A Memoir* (London, 1974).

24. Sir James Robertson, "Sovereign Nigeria," *African Affairs,* vol.59, no.239, April 1961, pp 145–154. Also, his *Transition in Africa: From Direct Rule to Independence—A Memoir* (London, 1974).

25. V Mckay, *Africa in World Politics* (2nd Edition, Westport, 1974), pp 399–400. Anthony Kirk-Greene identified three people who later occupied eminent positions in the Ministry of External and Commonwealth Affairs after independence. Isa Wali, G.H. Dove-Edwin and E.O. Sanu. See his *"Diplomacy and Diplomats: The Formation of Foreign Service Cadres in Black Africa,"* K Ingham, (ed.) *Foreign Relations of African States,* p 298.

26. FO371/146831: Sir Robert Scott to Foreign Office, July 4, 1960.

27. PS Gupta, *Imperialism and the British Labour Movement, 1914–1964* (London, 1975), pp 286–290. J Kent, *British Imperial Strategy and the Origin of the Cold War, 1944 -1949* (London, 1993).

28. DEFE7/415: Memorandum by Trafford Smith, October 24, 1951.

29. CAB129/69: Cabinet Memorandum by Lord Salisbury, July 24, 1954.

30. See David Goldsworthy, (ed.) British Documents on the end of empire: The Conservative Government-Part 1, pp 200–201.

31. CAB130/111: Note by Sir H. Parker, August 15, 1955.

32. DEFE7/1484: Nigeria Defence Agreement, 1960–1961. During the riots Awolowo was reported to have said that he along with Azikiwe, Balewa and Bello were forced to initiate the agreement in 1958. Evidence now points to the contrary. See *Senate Debates* (Nigeria), March—May 1960 session: 238; *Daily Times* (Nigeria) May 11, 1960; *Nigerian Tribune,* May 4, 1960; *House of Representatives Debates* (Nigeria), November 1960, p 61; IA Gambari, *Party Politics and Foreign Policy: Nigeria Under the First Republic* (Zaria, 1980), pp 33–53.

33. After 1947 Britain took a serious view of the implications of signing defence agreements with colonies before independence. This was a result of the USSR's criticism in the United Nations of the Anglo-Ceylon Defence Agreement signed before Ceylon's independence. The idea of defense pacts was thereafter postponed until after independence as in the case of Nigeria. Margaret Vogt wrongly asserts that the Anglo-Nigerian Defence Pact was signed in 1958. There was only a mutual consent on the part of the parties during the resumed Constitutional Conference in 1958. See Margaret Vogt, "Nigeria's Defence Policy: An Overview," in AE Ekoko, and M Vogt, (eds.) *Nigeria Defence Policy: Issues and Problems* (Lagos, 1990), p 95. Ekoko also missed the date when he stated that the pact was signed on the eve of independence. See Ekoko, A.E. "The Principles and Practices of Alliance Formation and Nigeria's Defence," in Ekoko and Vogt (eds.) *Nigeria.* In another study with Ajayi however, they both concluded that the pact was initialed in July 1960 and formerly signed on January 5, 1961. See JFA Ajayi, and AE Ekoko, "Transfer of Power in Nigeria: Its Origins and Con-sequences," Prosser Gifford, and Williams R. Louis, (eds.) *Decolonization and African Independence: The Transfers of Power in Africa, 1960–1980* (New Haven, 1988), p 263.

34. The British also viewed it in the same light. An official minutes that: "The greater our concern for the future security of Nigeria, the stronger is the reason for this predominantly pro-Western and friendly Government to give us what we are asking for under the Defence and stations of forces Agreement." See PREM11/3047: Nigeria—Defence Agreement Part 1, January 1960. It was reported that Awolowo even promised land in the Western Region to be used as the British base. See DEFE7/1484: Nigeria Defence Agreement . . . *op.cit;* Moreover, the first Nigerian Minister of Defence, Alhaji Muhammadu Ribadu viewed it as a "reaffirmation of the friendly and cordial ties which already exist and are known to exist between Nigeria and the United Kingdom." See *House of Representatives Debates* (Nigeria) November 1959, p 56.

35. CAB134/1353: Cabinet—Africa (Official) Committee: Prospects for the African Territories—Memorandum by the Colonial Office. Also see Draft Defence Agreement between the Government of the Great Britain and Northern Ireland and the Government of the Federation of Nigeria, *Sessional Paper* no.4, 1960.

36. Ibid, paragraph 24. Also CAB134/1353: Cabinet—Africa (Office) Committee: Future Constitutional Development in Colonies, p 5.

37. FO371/137972: Africa, paragraph 5 and 20.

38. Draft Defence Agreement . . . Article II, no.2, 3, 4, 5 and 6.

39. DEFE 7/1484: Nigeria Defence Agreement 1960–1961. Also, GJ Idang, "The Politics of Nigerian Foreign Policy: The Ratification and Renunciation of the Anglo-Nigerian Defence Agreement," *African Studies Review,* vol.xviii, no.2, September 1970, p 230.

40. This is discussed further on pages 258–274 in this chapter.

41. CS Phillips, *The Development of Nigerian Foreign Policy,* p 86.

42. Ibid, p. 72–77. GJ Idang, *Nigeria: Internal Politics and Foreign Policy,* pp 82–84.

43. *West African Pilot,* December 3, 1960; E Babatope, *Student Power in Nigeria, 1960—1970: A Documentary Sourcebook of Student Militancy in Nigeria, Volume 1* (Yaba, 1974), p 13; R Nassal, "Die Anfange der Kommunistichen Partei in Nigeria," *Internationales Afrika Forum,* 1, 4, April 1965, pp 25–29, is a detailed account of the Nigerian communists' role during the anti Anglo-Nigerian Defence Pact crisis after independence. I want to thank Monsieur Rufus Folaranmi, a teacher, translator and interpreter, of Strasbourg, France, for reading the article to me in the English language.

44. This is well analyzed by AE Hinds, "Sterling and imperial Policy, 1945–1951," *JICH,* Volume xv, no.2, January 1987, pp 148–169; "Imperial Policy and Colonial Sterling Balances, 1943–56," *JICH,* Volume xix, no.1, January 1991, pp 24–44. As it relates to Europe is analyzed by S Newton, "Britain, the Sterling Area and European Integration, 1945–1950," *JICH,* Volume xiii, no.3, May 1985, pp 163–182.

45. T Falola, (ed.) *Britain and Nigeria: Development or Under-Development?* G Williams, "Nigeria: A Political Economy," G Williams, (ed.) *Nigeria:*

Economy and Society (London, 1976), pp 1–54; and, Lawal, A.O. "British Commercial Interests and the Decolonization process in Nigeria, 1950–1960," *African Economic History*, 22, 1994, pp 93–110.

46. DJ Morgan, *The Official History—Volume Three*, pp 157–182.
47. Ibid.
48. CO967/203: Imperial Preference and the Sterling Area: Minutes by Sir H. Poynton, November 26, 1953.
49. Ibid.
50. D Goldsworthy, (ed.) *British Documents on the end of empire: The Conservative Government- Part III*, p 68.
51. CO967/203: Minutes by Sir H. Poynton; Also, Goldsworthy, *The Conservative Government*, pp 68–69.
52. Ibid.
53. Ibid.
54. CAB134/1353: Cabinet—Africa (Official) Committee: Future Constitutional Development, paragraph 28 (6).
55. CAB134/1353: Cabinet—Africa (Official) Committee: Prospects for the African Territories—Memorandum by the Colonial Office, paragraph 31.
56. DJ Morgan, *The Official History, Volume Three*, pp 211–232.
57. FO371/137972: Africa: The Next Ten Years: 20; See, Morgan, *The Official History . . . Volume Three*, pp 236–266.
58. CAB134/1353: Cabinet—Africa (Official) Committee: Minutes of Meeting -The Next Ten Years in Africa: West Africa, January 21, 1959, p 5.
59. Ibid, p 6.
60. CAB134/1353: Cabinet—Africa (Official) Committee: Technical Co-operation Scheme for Nigeria, February 20, 1959, p 1.
61. Ibid, p 1.
62. Ibid.
63. Ibid, p 2.
64. Ibid.
65. SP Schatz, *Nigerian Capitalism* (Berkeley/London, 1977); P Kirby, *Industrialization in an Open Economy: Nigeria 1945–1966* (Cambridge, 1969); J O'Connell, "The Political Class and Economic Growth," *Nigerian Journal of Economic and Social Studies*, Volume 8, March 1966.
66. *West African Pilot*, "Lift ban on Communist literature," October 20, 1960.
67. *Daily Express*, October 28, 1961.
68. Ibid.
69. CS Phillips, *The Development of Nigerian Foreign Policy* (London, 1964), p 61.
70. Records of All-Nigeria People's Conference, August 19–12, 1961, (Lagos: Nigerian Institute of International Affairs, 1961).
71. *West African Pilot*, September 26, 1964, p 1090.
72. *The Report of the Tribunal of Inquiry into the Activities of the Trade Union*, Lagos, 1977, p 41.
73. Ibid.
74. *West African Pilot*, February 7, 1964.

75. *Africa Diary,* September 1–7, 1962, p 735; *Africa Diary,* November 3–9, 1962.
67. Daily Express, October 28, 1961.
68. Ibid.
69. CS Phillips, The Development of Nigerian Foreign Policy (London, 1964), p 61.
70. Records of All-Nigeria People's Conference, August 19-12, 1961, (Lagos: Nigerian Institute of International Affairs, 1961).
71. West African Pilot, September 26, 1964, p 1090.
72. The Report of the Tribunal of Inquiry into the Activities of the Trade Union, Lagos, 1977, p 41.
73. Ibid.
74. West African Pilot, February 7, 1964.
75. Africa Diary, September 1-7, 1962, p 735; Africa Diary, November 3-9, 1962.

NOTES TO CHAPTER NINE

1. AJ Stockwell, (ed.) *British Documents on the end of Empire -Malaya, Part II: The Communist Insurrection, 1948–1953* (London: HMSO, 1992). Susan Carruthers has shown that Britain also engaged in a "wordy war" during the Malayan Emergency. See *Winning Hearts and Minds: British Governments, The Media and Colonial Counter-Insurgency, 1944–1960* (Leicester/London, 1995).
2. H Tijani, "McCarthyism in Colonial Nigeria," pp 645–668.
3. CP/CENT/INT/50/05: Idise Dafe, Report on Visit to Nigeria n.d. (but probably 1951), NMLHA, pp 1–7. Compare with Nkrumah's Gold Coast, Robert Young is of the view that there was a minimal Comintern and Profitern success. See RJC Young, *Postcolonialism: An Historical Introduction* (Massachusetts/Oxford, 2001), pp 226–230.
4. Ibid.
5. Ibid.
6. CP/CENT/INT/20/01: The Nigerian Commission 1950–1953; CP/CENT/INT/48/01: What Next in Nigeria? The National Movement and Political Parties 1954, NMLHA.
7. CP/CENT/INT/25/01: Samuel Ikoku, "Report on the Trade Union in Nigeria," autumn 1951, Manchester, UK.
8. See EB Idowu, *Olodumare: God in Yoruba Belief* (London, 1962); Ilogu, E. "Nationalism and the Church in Nigeria," *International Review of Missions,* 51, October 1962, pp 439–450; JFA Ajayi, *Christian Mission in Nigeria, 1841–1891* (London, 1970); EA Ayandele, *Missionary Impact on Modern Nigeria, 1842–1914* (London, 1974); TGO Gbadamosi, *The Growth of Islam in Yorubaland, 1841–1908* (London, 1978); SO Ilesanmi, *Religious Pluralism and the Nigerian State* (Athens, 1997).
9. AMCONGEN, Lagos to Department of State: Report on Northern Region Politics, 1953, File 745H.00/2–453, NARA, p 2.

10. A Bello, *My Life,* pp 236–237. Anthony Kirk-Greene has succinctly demonstrated this in his article, "His Eternity, His Eccentricity, or His Exemplarity? A Further Contribution to the Study of His Excellency, the African Head of State," *African Affairs,* vol.90, no.359, April 1991, pp 163–188. D Asaju, "The Politicisation of Religion in Nigeria," in S Johnson, (ed.) *Readings in Selected Nigerian Problems* (Lagos, 1990), p 181.

11. D Asaju, "The Politicisation of Religion," pp 181; Ilogu, E. "Nationalism and the Church in Nigeria," pp 439–450.

12. TP Melady, *Profiles of African Leaders* (New York, 1961), p 157.

13. A Foley, "Catholic and Communism," *Daily Comet* (Nigeria), October 30, 1948.

14. Ibid.

15. Mss292/File 966.3/4: Adebola to the Secretary-General, WFTU, Paris-France, October 23, 1952. Adebola was the secretary-General of the Railway Station Staff Union, Nigeria, as well as a Lagos representative at the Western House of Assembly.

16. Foley, "Catholic and Communism."

17. *Nigerian Catholic Herald,* October 29, 1948, Lagos. Also "Catholics and Communism—1948," Box A1 (IV) A-E, Marx Memorial Library, London.

18. *CACC Newsletter,* April/May 1961, 1–6

19. Ibid, 5

20. *West African Pilot,* January 18, 1951. An in depth study of the West African Pilot is contained in SO Idemili, "The West African Pilot and the movement for Nigerian nationalism 1937–1960," PhD Thesis, University of Wisconsin, Madison, 1980.

21. Ibid.

22. Willard Q. Stanton, Lagos to D.O.S.: Nigerian Anti-communist Editorial, December 6, 1950, File745.001/12–650, NARA.

23. Ibid. Also, *Nigerian Eastern Mail,* November 25, 1950.

24. *Nigerian Eastern Mail,* "The Invasion of Tibet," November 25, 1950.

25. CP/CENT/INT/25/01: Peoples Committee for Independence, Lagos, to Guiseppe Di Vittorio, President, WFTU, and Louis Saillant, General Secretary, WFTU, May 7, 1952, NMLH, p 8.

26. Interview with Anthony Kirk-Greene by the author, Oxford, March 1995. Details about the 1959 elections are in KWJ Post, *The Nigerian Federal Election of 1959: Politics and Administration in a Developing System* (Oxford, 1963).

27. A Kirk-Greene, (ed.) *Africa in the Colonial Period: The Transfer of Power - The Colonial Administrator in the Age of Decolonisation* (Oxford, 1979), pp 40–41; Sir James Robertson, "Sovereign Nigeria," *African Affairs,* vol.59, nos.239, April 1961.

28. CO 554/598: CO notes on the political beliefs of the three principal parties in Nigeria, March 1952, PRO.

29. CO 554/598: CO note, op cit; T Clark, *A Right Honourable Gentleman.*

30. N Eze, *"Memoir of a Crusader"* n.d.; I Nzimiro, *On Being a Marxist: The Nigerian Marxist and the Nigerian Revolution 1945–1952 (mimeo-*

graphed, Zaria, 1983); M Okoye, *The Beard of Prometheus*; SG Ikoku, *Nigerian History From a Socialist Viewpoint* (London, 1963); E Madunagu, *The Tragedy of the Nigerian Socialist Movement* (Port Harcourt, 1989). Scholars such as Apthorpe, Awa, Bhambri, Dudley, Frank, Omer-Cooper and Post, agree that the weakness of the proletariat to successfully challenge the control of the bourgeoisie during the colonial period was uppermost in their failure.

31. M Sherwood, *Kwame Nkrumah: The Years* Abroad, pp 151–153.
32. Ibid. p 130 and footnote 19.
33. OS Osoba, "Ideological Trends in the National Liberation." JAA Ayoade, "Party and Ideology in Nigeria: A case study of the Action Group," *Journal of Black Studies* 16 no. 2 (December, 1985).

Bibliography

UNPUBLISHED SOURCES:

(British) Trade Union Congress Collection, University of North London

Trade Union Congress Reports, 1947 to 1960—Reports of Proceedings at the Annual TUC Congresses in different parts of England.
TUC Colonial Advisory Committee Files, 1937 to 1953.
TUC International Committee Files I and III, Box 1853.
ICFTU Papers—Nigeria (General and Periodicals).
ICFTU Regional Office Weekly Newsletter, Accra, 1958–60.

Lyndon Baines Johnson Library, The University of Texas at Austin, USA

Communism—Africa: Communist Influence in the Federation of Nigeria, 1961.

Modern Record Centre, The University of Warwick, UK

These are TUC Registry Files 1941—1960.
Mss292/File 969.3/1, Nigeria, 1941–8.
Mss292/File 969.3/2, Nigeria, 1948–51.
Mss292/File 969.3/3, Nigeria, 1951–60.
Mss292/File 969.3/4, Nigeria, 1951–3.
Mss292/File 969.3/5, Nigeria, 1953–5.
Mss292/File 969.3/6, Nigeria, 1955–6.
Mss292/File 969.3/7, Nigeria, 1956–7.
Mss292/File 969.3/8, Nigeria, 1957–8.
Mss292/File 969.3/9, Nigeria, 1958–9.
Mss292/File 969.3/10, Nigeria, 1959.
Mss292/File 969.3/11, Nigeria, 1959–60.

Marx Memorial Library, Farringdon, London, UK

Pamphlet Box A1 (VI): Catholics and Communism—1948.
Pamphlet Box A1 (111) O–Z: Trade Unionism and Communism n.d.

Pamphlet Box A1 (111) O–Z: Theoretical Basis of Communism n.d.
Pamphlet Box A1 (VII) A–Z: Crisis of Britain and the British Empire—Marxist Study Theme no.7 1953.

Moral Re-armament Archives, Cheshire and Victoria, UK

"African Tail," A film by MRM, 1950.
"Freedom," A film by MRM, 1956.
MRA Information Service, vol.8, no.193, 1959.

Communist Party of Great Britain Papers, National Museum of Labour History Archive Centre, Manchester, UK

Papers of the Communist Party International Department; International Affairs Committee and External Relations; and individual files covering between 1948 and 1960 were read. In the Nigeria collections, the following files were read:
CP/IND/DUTT/09/10.
CP/ORG/1/9.
CP/CENT/ED/1/4.
CP/CENT/INT/19/01.
CP/CENT/INT/20/01.
CP/CENT/INT/20/02.
CP/CENT/INT/24/03.
CP/CENT/INT/24/04.
CP/CENT/INT/25/01.
CP/CENT/INT/25/04.
CP/CENT/INT/48/01.
CP/CENT/INT/50/03.
CP/CENT/INT/50/04.
CP/CENT/INT/50/05.
CP/CENT/INT/55/02.
CP/CENT/INT/55/03.
CP/CENT/INT/55/4.
CP/CENT/INT/55/05.
CP/CENT/INT/56/01.
The Labour Party Annual Reports, 1947–48.
The Labour Party Annual Reports, 1948–49.

Herbert Macaulay Papers, University of Ibadan Library, Nigeria

The Development of Political Parties in Nigeria.

National Archives Enugu, Nigeria

NSUDIV 8: Nsukka Division.

National Archives Ibadan, Nigeria

Apart from Government publications detailed below, these class files were used:

Comcol 1: Commissioner of the Colony.
CSO 26: Chief Secretary's Office.
Oyo Prof.1: Provincial Record.
MP/A4: Official/Unofficial (Prints) Publications (See "Government Publications" below for details).

National Archives and Record Administration, College Park, Maryland, USA

Apart from the State Department's publication titled: Foreign Relations of the United States (FRUS) 1945–1960, Consular records from US consulates in West Africa have been useful. Only file numbers are outlined here. These are Department of State record groups 59 and 84. They are grouped into central (decimal) files:

741.48; 741.48L; 848.00B; 848K and 848L.00B covering the period between 1945 through 1949.

641.45; 641.45H; 745.001 and 745H.001 covering the period between 1950 through 1960.

Nigeria Colonial Government Publications (National Archives Ibadan, Nigeria)

These are classified under MP/A4. They are:
Immigration Policy, 1950.
Criminal Code Ordinance 1950.
Unlawful Societies Act, Government Notice no.21, vol.37, April 1950.
Report of the Commission into the Disorder in the Eastern Provinces of Nigeria, no.256, 1950.
Foot Commission Report, 1950.
Phillipson, S. and Adebo, S.O. Nigeria: The Nigerianisation of the Civil Service—A Review of Policy Machinery, 1954.
Proposal for the establishment of the Nigerian Broadcasting Corporation, 1954.
Federation of Nigeria, Official Gazette, nos.57, October 1954.
Federation of Nigeria, Official Statement on the ban of the employment of communists in the Federal and Regional Public Service, Government Notice no.1769, 1954.
Laws of Nigeria, no.75, 1955.
Nigeria—Training of Nigerians for the representation of their country: A statement of policy by the Federal Government, 1957.
Report by Honourable Kolawole Balogun on his visit to the United States and Canada, Sessional paper no.2, 1958.
Department of Labour Annual Reports, 1945–1959, Government printers, Lagos, Nigeria.
Department of Labour Quarterly Review, 1946–1960.
Annual Reports of the Nigeria Police Force, 1945–1960, Government Printers, Lagos, Nigeria.
Nigeria: Views of the Government of the Federation on the Interim Report of the Committee on Nigerianisation, House of Representatives Sessional Paper no.7, 1958.

Board of Inquiry into the Trade Dispute Between the Elder Dempster Lines Limited and the Nigerian Union of Seamen Report, 1959.
House of Representatives Debates, 1956—1960.
Who is Who in Nigeria—A Biographical Dictionary, 1956.
Who is Who? House of Representatives, 1958.
House of Senate Debates, 1960.
Draft Defence Agreement Between the Government of the United Kingdom of Great Britain and Northern Ireland and the Government of the Federation of Nigeria, Sessional Paper no.4, 1960.
Guide to the Parliament of the Federation, 1960.

Public Record Office (The National Archive), Kew Gardens, London, UK
CAB 129: Cabinet Papers.
CAB 131: Defence Committee (Cabinet).
CAB 134: Africa Committee (Cabinet).
CO 537: West Africa—Supplementary Correspondence.
CO 554: West Africa—Original Correspondence.
CO 583: Nigeria—Original Correspondence.
CO 859: Colonial Office—Social Services Original Correspondence.
CO 968: International Relations and Defence—Original Correspondence.
CO 1039: Nigeria—Council of Ministers' Papers.
DEFE 7: Defence Committee (Ministry of Defence).
DEFE 11: Chief of Staff Secretariat Files.
FO 371: Foreign Office Correspondence.
PREM 11: Prime Minister's Papers.
WO 216: War Office Report on West Africa.

Harry S. Truman Library, Independence, Missouri, USA
President's Secretary File (PSF), Box 254-ORE1-1: Revised Soviet Tactics in International Affairs, January 6th 1947.
PSF, Box 254-ORE-28: The Break up of the colonial empires and its implications for US security, September 3rd 1948.
PSF Box 170, Message from Mr. Attlee to the President, July 6th 1950.
General File (GF), Box 477: Communism, 1951.
GF, Box 666: DuBois, W.E.B./Duckworth, 1951.
PSF/E.10501: A Report on the Strategic Ports of West Africa, March 1952.
PSF, Box 254/64: Probable Soviet Bloc Capabilities Through the mid-1953.
PSF, Box 254/64: Probable Soviet Course of Action, mid-1953.
PSF, Box 254/64: Soviet Block Capabilities Through mid-1954.

Rhodes House Library, Oxford, UK
Mss. Africa s.1477: Robertson's memo as Governor-General.
Mss. Africa s.1092: Interview of Robertson by Anthony Kirk-Greene.
Mss. Brit. Empr. S.332 Box 13 File 2—Nigeria 1955–1962.
Mss. Brit. Empr. S.332 Box 16 File 8—Nigeria and Sierra-Leone 1949.
Mss. Brit. Empr. S.332 Box 18 File 5—Lord Milverton 1947.

Mss. Brit. Empr. S.332 Box 18 File 6—Nigeria 1937–1965.
Mss. Brit. Empr. S.332 Box 45 File 2—Co-operation in the colonies 1943–1964.
Mss. Brit. Empr. S.332 Box 55 File 2—Nigeria 1950–1956.
Mss. Brit. Empr. S.365—Fabian Colonial Bureau Papers.

Royal Institute of International Affairs Library, London, UK
The following papers were read:
8/1675: Communism and the Church Today, April 5th 1949.
8/1892: Nigeria Today, July 26th 1950.
8/2064: The churches in the Face of communism, October 21st 1952.
8/2155: Communism and Islam, October 6th 1953.
8/2344: The Federation of Nigeria, October 20th 1955.
8/2470: The Political situation in Nigeria, 1956.
8/2773: Decolonisation—The Last stages, July 4th 1961.
8/2777: Nigeria, June 1961—July 27th 1961.

Funmilayo Ransome-Kuti (Anikulapo) Papers, University of Ibadan, Nigeria
Funmilayo Ransome-Kuti Diary 1952.
Funmilayo Ransome-Kuti Correspondence Boxes 1–5.
Solanke's Papers, Gandhi Library, University of Lagos, Akoka, Lagos, Nigeria:
Box 73, File 81, August 20th 1950.

Sopolu Library (Late Chief Obafemi Awolowo), Ikenne, Ogun State, Nigeria
Papers of the Action Group, Nigeria, 1952—1960.
Awolowo, O. "Anglo-Nigerian Military Pact Agreement," Action Group Bureau of
    Information, Lagos, 1960.

Newspapers and Magazines
The following newspapers are located at the British Newspapers' Library, Colin-
    dale, London; National Archives, Ibadan, Nigeria; the CPGB Archives in
    Manchester; TUC Collection and Registry Files in North London and War-
    wick; and National Archives and Record Administration, College Park,
    Maryland. Relevant newspapers/newsletters are:
African Bulletin (London).
African Labour (Accra).
African Newsletter (London).
Africa Report (Washington, D.C).
Christian Anticommunism Crusade Newsletter.
Daily Comet (Nigeria).
Daily Mirror (London).
Daily Service (Nigeria).
Daily Telegraph (London).
Daily Times (Nigeria).
Daily Worker (London).
Labour Champion (Nigeria).

Life Magazine (New York).
Manchester Guardian.
Nigerian Catholic Herald.
Nigerian Eastern Mail.
Nigerian Spokesman.
Nigerian Socialist Review.
Sunday Times (Nigeria).
The Christian Science Monitor (Boston).
The New York Times.
The Times (London).
West Africa (London).
West African Pilot (Nigeria).

Her Majesty's Stationery Office Publication, London, UK

Parliamentary Debates (Hansard), Fifth Series—House of Commons Official
    Report, 1947–1948; 1948–1949; House of Lords Official Reports, 1950.

Private Manuscripts

Eze, N. Memoirs of a Crusader, n.d.
Osita, A. Curriculum Vitae, An Abridged Version, Enugwu Ukwu, Enugu State,
    Nigeria, 1990.

Theses

H Adi, "West African Students and West African Nationalism in Britain,
    1900–1960," PhD History Thesis, University of London, 1994
SO Idemili, "The West African Pilot and the Movement for Nigerian Nationalism
    1937–1960," PhD Thesis, University of Wisconsin, Madison, 1980
AO Lawal, "Britain and the Decolonisation of Nigeria, 1945–1960," PhD History
    Thesis, University of Ibadan, Nigeria, 1992
R Melson, "Marxists in the Nigerian Labour Movement: A Case Study in the Fail-
    ure of Ideology," PhD Political Science Dissertation, Massachusetts Institute
    of Technology, 1967
R Kanet, "The Soviet Union and Sub-Saharan Africa: Communist Policy Toward
    Africa, 1917–1965," PhD Political Science Dissertation, Princeton University,
    1966
S Oyeweso, "The Political Thought of Mokwugo Okoye since 1950s," PhD History
    Thesis, Obafemi Awolowo University, Ile Ife, Nigeria, 1995
EO Rotimi, "A History of Native Administration Police Forces in Nigeria,
    1900–1970," PhD History Thesis, Obafemi Awolowo University, 1990
HI Tijani, "British anticommunist policies and the transfer of power in Nigeria
    from the late 1930s to 1960," MPhil. History Thesis, SOAS, University of
    London, 1998
HI Tijani, "Britain and the development of Leftist Ideology and Organisations in
    West Africa: The Nigerian Experience, 1945–1965," PhD History Thesis,
    University of South Africa, 2004

(B) PUBLISHED SOURCES

Selected Books

Adi, H, & Sherwood, M, *The 1945 Manchester Pan- African Congress Revisited* (London, 1995).

Adler, A, (ed.) *Theses, Resolutions, and Manifestos of the First Four Congresses of the Third International* (London, 1980)

Ahire, PT, *Imperial Policing: The Emergence and Role of the Police in Colonial Nigeria, 1860—1960* (London, 1991).

Ajala, A, *Pan-Africanism: Evolution, Progress and Prospects* (London, 1973).

Ajayi, JFA, & Crowder, M, (eds.) *History of West Africa, Vol. II* (2nd edition, London, 1987)

Akinjogbin, IA, & Osoba, SO, (eds.) *Topics on Nigerian Economic and Social History* (Ile Ife, 1980)

Albertini, RV, *Decolonization: The Administration and the Future of the Colonies, 1919–1960* (New York, 1971)

Albright, ED, *Africa and Communism* (London, 1960)

Akinyemi, AB, et. al (eds.) *International Relations—Nigeria Since Independence: The First 25 Years, Volume X* (Ibadan, 1989)

Akpala, A, *The Prospects of Small Trade Unions in Nigeria* (Enugu, 1963)

Aluko, O, *Ghana and Nigeria 1957—1970: A Study in Inter-African Discord* (London, 1976)

Amechi, M, *The Forgotten Heroes of Nigerian Independence* (Onitsha, 1985)

Ananaba, W, *The Trade Union Movement in Nigeria* (London, 1969)

Ananaba, W, *The Trade Union Movement in Africa: Promise and Performance* (London, 1979)

Anderson, DM, & Killingray, D, (eds.) *Policing and Decolonisation: Politics, Nationalism and the Police, 1917–1965* (Manchester, 1992)

Anyiam, FU, *Men and Matters in Nigerian Politics, 1934–1958* (Lagos, 1958)

Amenumey, DEK, *The Ewe Unification Movement: A Political History* (Accra, 1989)

Andrews, G, et al (eds.) *Opening the Books: Essays in the Social and Cultural History of Communism* (London, 1995)

Arikpo, O, *The Development of Modern Nigeria* (London, 1967)

Asante, SKB, *Pan-African Protests: West Africa and the Italo-Ethiopian Crisis, 1934–1941* (London, 1977)

Ashton, NJ, *Eisenhower, Macmillan and the Problem of Nasser: Anglo-American Relations and Arab Nationalism, 1955–1959* (London, 1996)

Ashton, S, & Stockwell, S, (eds.) *British Documents on the end of Empire: Imperial Policy and Colonial Practice, 1925–1945, Parts I & II* (London, 1996)

Awa, EO, Federal Government in Nigeria (Berkeley, 1964)

Awe, B, (ed.) *Nigerian Women in Historical Perspective* (Lagos, 1992)

Awolowo, O, Awo: An Autobiography of Chief Obafemi Awolowo (Cambridge, 1961)

Azikiwe, N, *My Odyssey* (London, 1970)

Azikiwe, N, *Zik: A Selection from the Speeches of Nnamdi Azikiwe* (Cambridge, 1961)

Azikiwe, N, *Ideology for Nigeria: Capitalism, Socialism or Welfarism?* (Lagos, 1980)

Babatope, E, *Student Power in Nigeria, 1960–1970: A Documentary Sourcebook of Student Militancy in Nigeria, Volume 1* (Yaba, 1974)

Babatope, E, *A Decade of Student Power in Nigeria 1960–1970* (Lagos, 1974)

Balogun, K, *My Country Nigeria* (Ibadan, 1971)

Black, CE, & Thornton, TP, (ed.) *Communism and Revolution—The Strategic Uses of Political Violence* (Princeton, 1964)

Bello, A, *My Life: An Autobiography of Sir Ahmadu Bello* (Cambridge, 1962)

Biobaku, S, *When We Were Young* (Ibadan, 1992)

Branson, N, *History of the Communist Party of Great Britain, 1927–1941* (London, 1987); *History of the Communist Party of Great Britain, 1941–1951* (London, 1997)

Brzezinski, Z, (ed.) *Africa and the Communist World* (Stanford, 1964).

Butler, LJ, *Industrialisation and the British Colonial State, West Africa 1939–1951* (London, 1997)

Cain, PJ, & Hopkins, AG, *British Imperialism: Crisis and Deconstruction 1914–1990* (London, 1993)

Carrauthers, S, *Winning Hearts and Minds: British Governments, The Media and Colonial Counter-Insurgency, 1944–1960* (Leicester/London, 1995)

Cell, J, *Hailey: A Study in British Imperialism, 1872–1969* (New York, 1992)

Clark, T, *A Right Honourable Gentleman—Abubakar From the Black Rock: A Narrative Chronicle of the Life and Times of Nigeria's Alhaji Sir Abubakar Tafawa Balewa* (London, 1991)

Clough, M, *US Policy Towards Africa and the end of the Cold War* (New York, 1992)

Cohen, P, *Children of the Revolution: Communist Childhood in Cold War Britain* (New York, 1997)

Cohen, R, *Labour and Politics in Nigeria* (2nd edition, London, 1981)

Coker, C, *NATO: The Warsaw Pact and Africa* (London, 1985)

Coleman, JS, *Nigeria: Background to Nationalism* (Berkeley, 1958)

Coleman, JS, *et. al* (eds.) *Political Parties and National Integration in Tropical Africa* (Los Angeles, 1964)

Condit, D, & Cooper, BH, (eds.) *Challenge and Response in Internal Conflict, vol.3* (Washington, D.C. 1968)

Cowan, EA, *A Trade Union Programme For Nigeria* (Lagos, 1953)

Crocker, WR, *Nigeria: A Critique of British Colonial Administration* (London, 1936)

Crowder, M, *The Story of Nigeria* (4th Edition, London, 1978)

Darwin, J, *The End of Empire* (London, 1991)

Davidson, AB, & Mazov, SV, (eds.) *Russia and Africa: Documents and Materials, XVIII Century—1960* (Moscow, 1999)

Davies, HO, *Memoirs* (Ibadan, 1989)

Delancey, M & Delancey, ELN, *Nigeria: A Bibliography of Politics, Government, Administration and Internal Relations* (Los Angeles, 1983)

Dockrill, M, & McKercher, B, (eds.) *Diplomacy and World Power: Studies in British Foreign Policy, 1890–1950* (Cambridge, 1996)

Dockrill, S, *Eisenhower's New Look National Security Policy, 1953–1961* (London, 1996)

Drachkovitch, MM, *Lenin and the Comintern, Volume 1* (Stanford, 1972)

Dunbabin, JPD, *International Relations Since 1945: The Cold War—The Great Powers and their Allies* (London, 1994)

Dunbabin, JPD, *International Relations Since 1945: The Post Imperial Age—The Great Powers and the Wider World* (London, 1994)

Dudley, BJ, *Parties and Politics in Northern Nigeria* (London, 1968)

Ekoko, AE, & Vogt, MA, (eds.) *Nigeria Defence Policy: Issues and Problems* (Lagos, 1990)

Elias, TO, *Nigeria: The Development of its Laws and Constitution* (London, 1967)

Emerson, R, *Africa and the United States Policy* (London, 1967)

Enahoro, A, *Fugitive Offender* (London, 1965)

Epelle, S, (ed.) *Nigeria Speaks: Speeches of Alhaji Sir Abubakar Tafawa Balewa* (Ikeja, 1964)

Esedebe, PO, *Pan-Africanism: The Idea and Movement, 1776–1963* (London, 1982)

Ezera, K, *Constitutional Developments in Nigeria* (Cambridge, 1960)

Falola, T, (ed.) *Britain and Nigeria: Development or Underdevelopment?* (New Jersey, 1987)

Falola, T, & Ihonvbere, J, (eds.) *Nigeria and the International Capitalist System* (Denver, 1988)

Falola, T, *Development Planning and Decolonization in Nigeria* (Florida, 1996)

Falola, T, (ed.) *Nigeria in the Twentieth Century* (Carolina Academic Press, 2002)

Falola, T, *Reforms and Economic Modernization in Nigeria* (Kent State University, 2004)

Feinstein, A, *African Revolutionary: The Life and Times of Nigeria's Aminu Kano* (London, 1987)

Fieldhouse, DK, *Merchant Capitals and Economic Decolonization: The United Africa Company 1929–1987* (Oxford, 1994)

Foot, H, *A Start in Freedom* (London, 1964)

Furedi, F, *Colonial Wars and the Politics of Third World Nationalism* (London, 1994)

Gambari, IA, *Party Politics and Foreign Policy: Nigeria Under the First Republic* (Zaria, 1980)

Gifford, P, & Louis, WR, (eds.) *The Transfer of Power in Africa: Decolonization, 1940–1960* (New Haven, 1982)

Gifford, P, & Louis, WR, (eds.) *Decolonization and African Independence: The Transfers of Power in Africa, 1960–1980* (New Haven, 1988)

Goldsworthy, D, (ed.) *British Documents on the end of Empire: The Conservative Government and the end of Empire, Parts I, II & III* (London, 1994)

Grace, J, & Laffin, J, (eds.) Fontana Dictionary of Africa Since 1960 (London, 1991)

Gupta, PS, *Imperialism and the British Labour Movement, 1914–1964* (London, 1975)

Hailey, WM, *Native Administration in British African Territories, Part 3, West Africa* (London, 1951/Nendeln, 1979)

Hailey, WM, *An African Survey: A Study of Problems Arising in Africa South of the Sahara* (Revised edition, London, 1957)

Haines, CG, (ed.) *The Threat of Soviet Imperialism* (Baltimore, 1954)

Hammonds, TT, & Farrell, R, (eds.) *The Anatomy of Communist Takeovers* (New Haven, 1975)

Harding, N, *Leninism* (Durham, 1996).

Hargreaves, JD, *Decolonization in Africa* (London, 1988)

Havinden, M, & Meredith, D, *Colonialism and Development: Britain and its Tropical Colonies, 1850–1960* (New York, 1996)

Haynes, JE, *Red Scare or Red Menace?—American Communism and Anticommunism in the Cold War Era* (Chicago, 1996)

Heinlein, F, British government policy and decolonisation, 1945–1963: Scrutinising the official mind (London, 2002)

Hinden, R, Socialism and the Colonial World (London, 1959)

Hobsbawn, E, *Age of Extreme—The Short Twentieth Century, 1914–1991* (London, 1994)

Hodgkin, T. *African Political Parties* (Reprinted, Baltimore, 1971)

Holland, RF, *European Decolonization 1918–1981: An Introductory Survey* (Basingstoke, 1985)

Hooker, JR, *Black Revolutionary: George Padmore's Path From Communism to Pan-Africanism* (London, 1967)

Howe, S, *Anticolonialism in British Politics: The Left and the end of Empire, 1918–1964* (Oxford, 1993)

Hue-Tam, HT, *Radicalism and the Origins of the Vietnamese Revolution* (Cambridge, 1992)

Hughes, A, (ed.) *Marxism's Retreat From Africa* (London, 1992)

Hyam, R, (ed.) *British Documents on the end of Empire: The Labour Government and the end of Empire, Part I, II, III & IV* (London, 1994)

Hyam, R, & Louis, WR, (eds.) The conservative government and the end of empire, 1957–1964: Parts I & II (London, 2000)

Idang, GJ, *Nigeria: Internal Politics and Foreign Policy, 1960–1966* (Ibadan, 1973)

Igwe, A, *Nnamdi Azikiwe: The Philosopher of Our Time* (Enugu, 1992)

Ikime, O, (ed.) *Groundwork of Nigerian History* (London, 1982)

Ikoku, SG, *Nigeria for Nigerians: A Study of Contemporary Nigerian Politics From a Socialist Point of View* (Takoradi, 1962)

Ilesanmi, SO, *Religious Pluralism and the Nigerian State* (Athens, 1997)

Inghram, K, (ed.) *Foreign Relations of African States: Colston Paper No. 25* (London, 1974)

Iweriebor, EEG, *Radical Politics in Nigeria, 1945–1950: The Significance of the Zikist Movement* (Zaria, 1996)

Johnson, S, (ed.) *Readings in Selected Nigerian Problems* (Lagos, 1990)

Johnson-Odim, C, & Mba, NE, *For Women and the Nation: Funmilayo Ransome-Kuti of Nigeria* (Urbana, 1997)

Johnston, D, & Sampson, C, (ed.) *Religion, The Missing Dimension of Statecraft* (Oxford, 1994)

Joseph, RA, *Radical Nationalism in Cameroun—Social Origins of the U.P.C. Rebellion* (Oxford, 1977)

July, R, *An African Voice: The Role of the Humanities in African Independence* (Durham, 1987)

Kaplan, MA, (ed.) *The Many Faces of Communism* (New York, 1978)

Kent, J, *The Internationalization of Colonialism: Britain, France and Black Africa, 1939–1956* (Oxford, 1992)

Kent, J, *British Imperial Strategy and the Origin of the Cold War, 1944–1949* (London, 1993)

Killingray, D, & Rathbone, R, (eds.) *Africa and the Second World War* (London, 1986)

Kirby, P, *Industrialization in an Open Economy: Nigeria 1945–1966* (Cambridge, 1969)

Kirk-Greene, AH, (ed.) *Africa in the Colonial Period: The Transfer of Power—The Colonial Administrator in the Age of Decolonisation* (Oxford, 1979)

Kolakowski, L, *Main Currents of Marxism—Volume 3* (Oxford, 1981)

Langley, JA, *Pan-Africanism and Nationalism in West Africa, 1900–1945: A Study in Ideology and Social Class* (Oxford, 1973)

Laybourn, K, *A History of British Trade Unionism* (Sutton, 1996)

Laybourn, K, *The Rise of Socialism in Britain* (Sutton, 1997)

Legum, C, *Pan-Africanism: A Short Political Guide* (London, 1965)

Legvoid, R, *Soviet Policy in West Africa* (Cambridge, 1970)

Lockwood, SB, *Nigeria: A Guide to Official Publications* (Library of Congress, Washington, D.C. 1966)

Louis, WR, & Bull, H, (eds.) *The Special Relationship: Anglo-American Relations Since 1945* (Oxford, 1986)

Lynn, M, *British Documents on the end of empire: Nigeria, Parts 1 & 2* (London, 2001)

Mackenzie, JM, *Propaganda and Empire: The Manipulation of British Public Opinion, 1880—1960* (Manchester, 1984)

Mackenzie, JM, (ed.) *Imperialism and Popular Culture* (Manchester, 1986)

Madunagu, E, *The Tragedy of the Nigerian Socialist Movement* (Calabar, 1980)

Maliki, K, *The Meaning of Race: Race, History and Culture in Western Society* (London, 1996)

Matusevich, M, *No Easy Row for a Russian Hoe: Ideology and Pragmatism in Nigerian-Soviet Relations, 1960–1991* (Trenton, 2003)

Mayer, A, *Wilson vs. Lenin: Political Origins of the New Diplomacy, 1917–1918* (New York, 1967)

Mba, NE, *Nigerian Women Mobilised* (Berkeley, 1982)

Mbadiwe, KO, *Rebirth of a Nation* (Enugu, 1991)

McIntyre, W, *Background to the ANZUS: Policy Making, Strategy and Diplomacy, 1945–1955* (Canterbury, 1995)

Mckay, V, *Africa in World Politics* (2nd edition, Westport, 1974)

Melady, TP, *Profiles of African Leaders* (New York, 1961)

Mellanby, K, *The Birth of Nigeria's University* (London, 1958)

Morgan, JD, *The Official History of Colonial Development, 5vols;* (London, 1980)

Morris-Jones, WH, & Fisher, G, (eds.) *Decolonisation and After: The British and French Experience* (London, 1980)

Myers, RA, *World Bibliographic Series: Nigeria—Volume 100* (Oxford, 1989)

Nicholson, IF, *The Administration of Nigeria: Methods and Myths, 1900–1960* (London, 1969)

Nicholson, M, *The TUC Overseas—The Roots of Policy* (London, 1986)

Nkrumah, K, Revolutionary Path (London, 1964); Handbook of Revolutionary Warfare: A Guide to the Armed Phase of the Africa Revolution (London, 1968); Consciencism: Philosophy and Ideology for Decolonization (New York, 1964)

Nogee, JL, & Donaldson, RH, *Soviet Foreign Policy Since World War II* (New York, 1988)

Nove, A, *The Soviet Economic System* (2ⁿᵈ Impression, London, 1978)

Nzimiro, I, *On Being a Marxist: The Nigerian Marxists and the Nigerian Revolution, 1945–1952* (Zaria, 1983)

Offodile, C, *Dr. M.I. Okpara: A Biography* (Enugu, 1980)

Okonkwo, R, *Protest Movements in Lagos, 1908—1930* (New York, 1995)

Okoye, M, *The Beard of Prometheus* (Bristol, 1965)

Okoye, M, *A Letter to Dr. Nnamdi Azikiwe: A Dissent Remembered* (Enugu, 1979)

Okoye, M, *Embattled Men—Profiles in Social Adjustment* (Enugu, 1980)

Olisa, MSO, *et. al;* (eds.) *Azikiwe and the African Revolution* (Onitsha, 1989)

Olusanya, GO, *The Second World War and Politics in Nigeria, 1939–1953* (London, 1973)

Olusanya, GO, *The West African Students' Union and the Politics of Decolonisation, 1925–1958* (Lagos, 1982)

Oluwide, B, *Imoudu Biography Part 1—A Political History of Nigeria 1939–1950* (Ibadan, 1993)

Otobo, D, *Foreign Interest and Nigerian Trade Unions* (Ibadan, 1986)

Otobo, D, *State and Industrial Relations in Nigeria* (Ibadan, 1988)

Oyebade, A, (ed.) *The Foundations of Nigeria: Volume II* (Trenton, 2003)

Ovendale, R, *British Defence Policy Since 1945* (Manchester, 1994)

Oyelaran, OO, *et. al;* (eds.) *Obafemi Awolowo: The End of an Era ?* (Ile Ife, 1988)

Oyeweso, S. *Mokwugo Okoye: Struggle for National Liberation and Social Justice* (Lagos: Multivision, 2003)

Paden, JN, *Ahmadu Bello—Sardauna of Sokoto: Values and Leadership in Nigeria* (London, 1986)

Padmore, G, *Communism or Pan-Africanism?: The Coming Struggle for Africa* (London, 1956)

Patsouraus, L, & Thomas, JR, (eds.) *Varieties and Problems of Twentieth -Century Socialism* (Chicago, 1981)

Pearce, R, *The Turning Point in Africa* (London, 1982)

Phillips, CS, (Jnr.) *The Development of Nigerian Foreign Policy* (Evanston, 1964)

Pierson, S, *Marxism and the Origins of British Socialism—The Struggle for a New Consciousness* (Ithaca, 1973)

Porter, AN, & Stockwell, AJ, *British Imperial Policy and Decolonisation, vol.1, 1938-1951* (London, 1987)

Porter, AN, & Stockwell, AJ, *British Imperial Policy and Decolonisation, vol. 2, 1951-1964* (London, 1989)

Porter, AN, (ed.), *Oxford History of the British Empire, vol. 3, The 19th Century* (Oxford University Press, 1999)

Post, KWJ, *The Nigerian Federal Election of 1959: Politics and Administration in a Developing System* (Oxford, 1963)

Powaski, RE, *The Cold War: The United States and the Soviet Union, 1917-1991* (Oxford, 1997)

Rathbone, R, (ed.) *British Documents on the end of Empire: Ghana, Parts 1 & 2* (London, 1992)

Rich, P, *Race and Empire in British Politics* (Cambridge, 1986)

Roberts, AD, (eds.) *The Colonial Moment in Africa: Essays on the Movement of Minds and Materials, 1900-1940* (Cambridge, 1990)

Robertson, J, *Transition in Africa: From Direct Rule to Independence—A Memoir* (London, 1974)

Royal Institute of International Affairs: *Nigeria—The Political and Economic Background* (London, 1960).

Royle, T, *Winds of Change in Africa: The End of Empire in Africa* (London, 1996)

Seldon, M, & Lippit, V, (eds.) *The Transition to Socialism in China* (New York, 1982)

Schatten, F, *Communism in Africa* (London, 1966)

Schatz, SP, *Nigerian Capitalism* (Berkeley, 1977)

Schrecker, E, *The Age of McCarthyism: A Brief History with Documents* (Boston, 1994)

Schrecker, E, *No Ivory Tower: McCarthyism and the Universities* (New York, 1986)

Sherwood, M, *Kwame Nkrumah: The Years Abroad, 1935-1947* (Legon, 1996)

Sills, D, (ed.) *International Encyclopeadia of the Social Sciences, Volumes 3 & 10* (London, 1968)

Silva, KM, (ed.) *British Documents on the end of Empire: Sri Lanka, 2vols;* (London, 1997)

Sklar, R, *Nigerian Political Parties: Power in an Emergent African Nation* (Princeton, 1963)

Smith, BS, *But Always as Friends: Northern Nigeria and the Cameroons, 1912-1957* (London, 1969)

Smith, J, (ed.) *Administering Empire: The British Colonial Service in Retrospect* (London, 1999)

Smith, T, (ed.) *The End of the European Empire: Decolonization after World War II* (London, 1975)

Smock, DR, *Conflict and control in African trade union: a study of the Nigerian coal miners union* (Stanford, 1969)

Steinberg, PL, *The Great "Red Menace": United States Prosecution of American Communists, 1947-1952* (Connecticut, 1984)

Stevens, C, *The Soviet Union and Black African* (London, 1976)

Stockwell, AJ, (ed.) *British Documents on the end of the Empire: Malaya, Part I, II and III* (London, 1996)

Tamuno, TN, *The Police in Modern Nigeria, 1861—1960* (Ibadan, 1970)
Tamuno, TN, *The Evolution of the Nigerian State: The Southern Phase, 1898–1914* (London, 1972)
Thorpe, A, *The British Communist Party and Moscow 1920–1943* (Manchester, 2000)
Tokunboh, MA, *Labour Movement in Nigeria: Past and Present* (Lagos, 1985)
Usman, YB, & Kwanashie, GA, (eds.) *Inside Nigeria History 1950–1970: Events, Issues and Sources* (Ibadan, 1995)
Uyilawa, U, *The Rise and Fall of the Zikist Movement, 1946–1950* (Lagos, 1983)
Walker, M, *The Cold War and the Making of the Modern World* (London, 1993)
Wesson, RG, *Communism and Communist Systems* (New Jersey, 1978)
Westoby, A, *The Evolution of Communism* (Oxford, 1989)
White, JJ, *Central Administration in Nigeria, 1914–1951* (London, 1981)
Williams, G, (ed.) *Nigeria: Economy and Society* (London, 1976)
Wilson, ET, *Russia and Black Africa Before World War II* (London, 1974)
Wilson, HS, Origins of Wes African Nationalism (London, 1969)
Wilson, HS, *African Decolonisation* (London, 1994)
Yesufu, TM, *An Introduction to Industrial Relations in Nigeria* (London, 1962)
Young, RJC, Postcolonialism: An Historical Introduction (Massachusetts/ Oxford, 2001)
Zachernuk, P. *Colonial Subjects: An African Intelligentsia and Atlantic Ideas* (Virginia, 2000)

Selected Articles in Learned Journals

Abdul Raheem, T, & Olukoshi, A, "The Left in Nigerian Politics and the struggle for socialism, 1945—1986," *Review of African Political Economy, no.37,* 1986
Adie, WAC, "The Communist Powers in Africa," *Conflict Studies, No. 10,* December—January 1970/71.
Allen, RB, "Communists should not teach in American Colleges," *Educational Forum,* vol.13, no.4, May 1949
Aluko, O, "Foreign Service," *Quarterly Journal of Administration,* no.5, 1970
Aluko, O, "The Organisation and the Administration of the Nigerian Foreign Service," *Ife International Relations, Occasional Papers 1,* July 1981.
Amin, S, "Marxism," *Monthly Review,* vol.26, no.2, June 1974
Apthorpe, R, "Opium of the State—Some Remarks on Law and Society in Nigeria," *The Nigerian Journal of Economic and Social Studies,* 6, 2, July 1964
Armour, C, "The BBC and the development of broadcasting in British colonial Africa, 1946—1956," *African Affairs,* vol.83, no.322, July 1984
Awa, EO, "The Place of Ideology in Nigerian Politics," *African Review: A Journal of African Politics, Development and International Affairs,* 4, 3, 1974
Ayoade, JAA, "Party and Ideology in Nigeria: A Case of the Action Group," *Journal of Black Studies* 16 no. 2 (December, 1985)
Bhambri, RS, "Marxist Economic Doctrines and their Relevance to Problems of Economic Development of Nigeria," *The Nigerian Journal of Economic and Social Studies,* 6, 2, July 1964

Carew, A, "Charles Millard, A Canadian in the International Labour Movement: A Case Study of the ICFTU 1955–1961," *Labour/Le Travail*, 37 (Spring, 1996)

Cell, JW, "On the eve of Decolonisation: The Colonial Office's Plans for the Transfer of Power in Africa, 1947," *Journal of Imperial and Commonwealth History, vol.viii, no.3,* May 1980

Crawley, AM, "Communism and African Independence," *African Affairs*, vol.64, no.255, April 1965

Dudley, BJ, "Marxism and Political Change in Nigeria," *The Nigerian Journal of Economic and Social Studies*, 6, 2, July 1964

Egboh, EO, "Central Trade Unionism in Nigeria (1941–1966)," *Geneve Afrique*, vol.vi—no.2, 1967

Egboh, EO, "The Early Years of Trade Unionism in Nigeria," *Africa Quarterly*, vol.viii, no.1, April–June 1968

Eluwa, GIC, "The National Congress of British West Africa: A Pioneer Nationalist Movement," *Tarikh*, vol.3, no.4, 1981

Frank, LP, "Ideological Competition in Nigeria: Urban Populism versus Elite Nationalism," *Journal of Modern African Studies*, 17, 3, September 1979

Friedland, WH, "Organizational Chaos and Political Potential," *Africa Report*, vol.10, no.6, June 1965

Furlong, PJ, "Azikiwe and the National Church of Nigeria and the Cameroons: A case study of Religion in African Nationalism," *African Affairs*, vol.91, no.364, July 1992

Goldsworthy, D, "Keeping Change within Bounds: Aspects of Colonial Policy During the Churchill and Eden Governments, 1951–56," *Journal of Imperial and Commonwealth History*, vol.xviii, no.1, January 1990

Gonidec, PF, "The Development of Trade Unionism in Black Africa," *Bulletin of the Inter-African Labor Institute*, vol.x, no.2, May 1963

Gorman, R, "Soviet Perspectives on the Prospects for Socialist Development in Africa," *African Affairs*, vol.83, no.331, April 1984

Hennings, J, "The Attitudes of African Nationalism Towards Communism," *Duquesque University Institute of African Affairs*, no.10, 1961

Hinds, AE, "Sterling and Imperial Policy, 1945–1951," *Journal of Imperial and Commonwealth History*, vol.xv, no.2, January 1987

Hinds, AE, "Imperial Policy and Colonial Sterling Balances, 1943–56," *Journal of Imperial and Commonwealth History*, vol.xix, no.1, January 1991

Hodson, HV, "Race Relations in Commonwealth," *International Affairs*, vol.26, July 1950

Holland, R, (ed.) Special Issue: Emergencies and Disorder in the European Empires After 1945, *Journal of Imperial and Commonwealth History*, vol.xxi, no.3, September 1993

Idang, G, "The Politics of Nigerian Foreign Policy: The Ratification and Renunciation of the Anglo-Nigerian Defence Agreement," *African Studies Review*, vol.xiii, no.2, September 1970

Ilogu, E, "Nationalism and the Church in Nigeria," *International Review of Missions*, 51, October 1962

Joseph, RA, "National Politics in Post-war Cameroun: The Difficulty Birth of the U.P.C.," *Journal of African Studies,* vol.II, no.2, 1975

Killingray, D, "The Maintenance of Law and Order in British colonial Africa," *African Affairs,* vol.85, no.340, July 1986

Kirk-Greene, AHM, "The New African Administrator," *Journal of Modern African Studies,* vol.x, no.1, 1972

Kirk-Greene, AHM, "His Eternity, His Eccentricity, or His Exemplarity? A Further Contribution to the Study of His Excellency the African Head of State," *African Affairs,* vol.90, no.359, April 1991

Klinghoffer, AJ, "The Soviet View of African Socialism," *African Affairs,* vol.67, no.268, July 1968

Kent, J, "Anglo-French Colonial Co-operation, 1939–1949," *Journal of Imperial and Commonwealth History,* vol.xvii, no.1, October 1988

Lawal, AO, "British Commercial Interests and the Decolonization Process in Nigeria, 1959–1960," *African Economic History,* 22, 1994

Lee, JM, "'Forward Thinking' and War: The Colonial Office During the 1940s," *Journal of Imperial and Commonwealth History,* vol.vi, no.1, October 1977

Legum, C, "Pan-Africanism: The Communists and the West," *African Affairs,* vol.63, no.252, July 1964

Leo, S, & Denzer, L, "I.T.A. Wallace Johnson and the West African Youth League," *Journal of African Historical Studies,* vol.6, no.3–4, 1973

Lichtblau, GE, "The Communist Labor Offensive in former Colonial Countries," *Industrial and Labor Relations Review,* vol.15, no.3, April 1962

Lichtblau, GE, "The Dilemma of the ICFTU," *Africa Report,* vol.10, no.6, June 1965

Lorwin, LL, "Communism," *The Encyclopeadia Americana,* International Edition, Vol.7 (New York, 1977)

Louis, WR, "American Anti-colonialism and the dissolution of the British Empire," *International Affairs,* 61, 1985

Lynn, M, "The Eastern crisis of 1955–57, the Colonial Office and Nigerian Decolonisation," *Journal of Imperial and Commonwealth History,* 30 (2002)

Matrey, F, "Socialism and National Liberation Movement in Africa, 1917–1939," *African Studies in the Soviet Union,* 1990/91

Metz, S, "American Attitudes Toward Decolonization in Africa," *Political Science Quarterly,* Fall 84, vol.99 Issue 3

Morison, D, "The Africa of Moscow and Peking—A Review Article," *African Affairs,* vol.66, no.265, October 1967

Narasingha, S, "Nigeria Intellectuals and Socialism: Retrospect and Prospect," *Journal of Modern African Studies,* 31, 3, 1993

Nassal, R, "Die Anfange der Kommunistichen Partei in Nigeria," *Internationales Afrika Forum,* 1, 4, April 1965

Nelkin, D, "The Search for Continental Unity," *Africa Report,* vol.10, no.6, June 1965

Northedge, FS, "East-West Relations: Detente and After," *Institute of Administration Monographs Series,* no.4, University of Ife (now Obafemi Awolowo), 1974

O'Connell, J, "The Political Class and Economic Growth," *Nigerian Journal of Economic and Social Studies,* vol.8, March 1966

Ojedokun, O, "The Anglo-Nigerian Entente and its Demise, 1960–1962," *Journal of Commonwealth Political Studies,* vol.ix, no.3, November 1971

Ojedokun, O, "The Changing Pattern of Nigeria's International Economic Relations: The Decline of the colonial Nexus, 1960–1966," *Journal of Developing Nations,* July 1972

Olusanya, GO, "The Zikist Movement—A Study in Political Radicalism, 1946–1950," *Journal of Modern African Studies,* 4, 1966

Olusanya, GO, "Nigeria and East-West Relations," *Nigerian Forum,* January/February, 1990

Omer-Cooper, JD, "Nigeria, Marxism and Social Progress—An Historical Perspective," *Nigerian Journal of Economic and Social Studies,* 6, 2, July 1964

Osita, A, "A Call for Revolution and the Forgotten Heroes: The Story of the Zikist Movement of 1948," *Journal of the Association of Francophone Studies,* vol.1, no.1, 1990

Osoba, OS, "Ideological Trends in Nigerian National Liberation Identity, Solidarity and Motivation, 1935–1965: A Preliminary Assessment," *Ibadan,* no.27, October 1969

Oyebade, A, "Feeding America's War Machine: The United States and Economic Expansion in West Africa During World War II," *African Economic History,* 26, (1998)

Oyemakinde, WO, "The Nigerian General Strike of 1945," *Journal of the Historical Society of Nigeria,* 7, 4, June 1975

Parsons, S, "British Communist Party School Teachers in the 1940s and 1950s," *Science and Society, Special Issue,* Spring 1997

Pearce, RD, "Governors, Nationalists and the Constitution in Nigeria, 1935–1951," *Journal of Imperial and Commonwealth History,* vol.ix, no.3, May 1981

Pearce, RD, "The Colonial Office in 1947and the Transfer of Power in Africa: An Addendum to John Cell," *Journal of Imperial and Commonwealth History,* vol.x, no.2, January 1982

Post, KWJ, "Nationalism and Politics in Nigeria: A Marxist Approach," *Nigerian Journal of Economic and Social Studies,* 6, 2, July 1964

Redfern, N, "British Communists, the British Empire and the Second World War," *International Labor and Working Class History,* No. 65, Spring 2004

Richards, Y, "Race, Gender, and Anticommunism in the International Labor Movement: The Pan-African Connections of Maida Springer," *Journal of Women's History* 11, 2, 1999

Roberts, M, "African Trade Unionism in Transition," *The World Today,* vol.17, no.10, October 1961

Robertson, J, "Sovereign Nigeria," *African Affairs,* vol.59, no.239, April 1961

Robinson, R, "The Moral Disarmament of African Empire, 1919–1947," *Journal of Imperial and Commonwealth History,* vol. III, no.1, October 1979

Sherwood, M, "The CPGB, the colonies and Black Britons," *Science and Society,* 60 (1996)

Stevens, C, "Africa and the Soviet Union," *International Relations,* 3, 12, November 1971

Tamuno, T, "The Independence Movement in Nigeria," *Tarikh,* vol.4, no.1, Second Impression, 1977

The African Communist, Editorial comment: "African Martyr—Ernest Quandie," *African Communist,* 46, Third Quarter, 1971

Tingwey, PF, "Communism and Cameroon," *The Kamerun Student,* 4, May 1965

Waterman, P, "Communist Theory in the Nigerian Trade Union Movement," *Politics and Society,* 3, 3, 1973

Williams, MW, "Nkrumahism as an Ideological Embodiment of Leftist Thought Within the African World," *Journal of Black Studies* 15, no. 1 (September, 1984)

WZC, (Initials used) "Nasserism and Communism," *The World Today,* vol.12, no.9, September 1956

Zakharia, I, & Magigwana, C, "The Trade Unions and the Political Scene in Africa," *World Marxist Review,* December 1964

Index